CROSSBILL GUIDES

The nature guide to
Extremadura

SPAIN

ISBN 90 5011 223 4

The Nature Guide to Extremadura
© Crossbill Guides Foundation, Nijmegen / The Netherlands and KNNV Publishing, Utrecht / The Netherlands, 2006.
www.crossbillguides.org
www.knnvpublishing.nl

Initiative, text and research: Dirk Hilbers
Editing: Dorri te Boekhorst, Barbara Kwast, Manuela Seifert, Cees Hilbers, Riet Hilbers, Brian Redekopp
Additional editing, text and research: Kim Lotterman
Language suggestions: Brian Redekopp
Illustrations: Horst Wolter, Chris Braat
Lay-out: Gert Jan Bosgra

Print: Ponsen en Looijen, Wageningen

For more information and to order, visit us at www.crossbillguides.org

This book is published in association with KNNV Publishing, The Netherlands and with financial support of DOEN Foundation, The Netherlands.

KNNV Publishing

CROSSBILL
GUIDES
FOUNDATION

This guidebook is a product of the non-profit foundation Crossbill Guides. By publishing these books we want to introduce more people to the joys of Europe's beautiful natural heritage and to increase the understanding of the ecological values that underlie conservation efforts. Most of this heritage is protected for ecological reasons and we want to provide insight into these reasons to the public at large. By doing so we hope that more people support the ideas behind nature conservation.
For more information about us and our guides you can visit our website at:

WWW.CROSSBILLGUIDES.ORG

4

About this guide

This guide is meant for all those who enjoy being in and learning about nature, whether you already know all about it or not. It is set up a bit differently than most guides. We focus more on explaining the natural and ecological features of an area than on merely describing it. We choose this approach because to us nature in an area is more interesting, more enjoyable and more valuable when seen in the context of its internal relationships. The continuous interplay of different species with each other and with their environment is simply mind-blowing. The clever tricks and gimmicks that are put to use to beat life's challenges are countless.

Take the crossbill, for example: at first glance just a big finch with a funny bill. But there is more to the crossbill than meets the eye. This bill is actually an adaptation to the environment in which the bird lives: pine forests. The bill is used like a pair of scissors to cut open pinecones and eat the seeds that are unreachable for other birds. Especially in the Scandinavian countries where pine and spruce take up the greater part of the forests, several crossbill species have managed to answer one of life's most pressing questions: how to get food. By evolving a crossed bill they have secured their place in the arena for survival. Now this should heighten the appreciation of what at first glance was merely a fat red bird with a beak that doesn't close properly. Once its interrelationships are seen, nature comes alive, wherever you are.

Unfortunately, many people still feel that although European nature is great for a leisurely stroll, it remains a puny surrogate of the wilderness of the Amazon, the vastness of the Serengeti or the sublimity of Yellowstone. If you haven't seen a lion, you haven't seen real nature, is in short the argument. Nonsense, of course.

But where to go? And how? What is there to see? That is where this guide comes in. We describe the how, the why and the where of Europe's most beautiful areas. In clear and accessible language, we explain Extremadura and refer extensively to routes where the area's features can be observed best. We try to make Extremadura come alive. We hope that we succeed.

How to use this guide

This guidebook contains a descriptive and a practical section. The descriptive comes first and gives you insight into the most interesting, remarkable and beautiful natural gems of the area. It gives an understanding of what you will see when exploring the field. The second part offers, apart from some practical information on what you should and should not do, suggestions on routes that are interesting to follow. To cater to everyone, we have included not only walks, but also bicycle routes and car trips.
A number of icons give a quick overview of the characteristics of each route. These icons are explained in the margin of this page.
Using this guide is as easy as a walk in the park. There is no need to start reading on page one so that you finally know where you can go once you have reached page fifty a day later. Instead, each small chapter stands on its own and refers to the routes most suitable for viewing the particular features described in it. Conversely, descriptions of each route refer to the chapters that explain the most typical features that can be seen along the way.
We try to keep the number of scientific terms to a minimum. If using one is unavoidable, we explain it in the glossary at the end of the guide. There we have also included a list of plant and animal species, including their scientific names and translations into German and Dutch.
Some of these names have an asterisk (*) behind them. This indicates that there is no official English name for this species and that we have taken the liberty of coining one. We realise that this will meet with some reservation with those who are well up on scientific names. For the sake of readability, however, we have decided to translate the scientific name.
Please note that we do not want to claim these names as the new official English names. We merely want to facilitate a smoother reading for the greater public.
An overview of Extremadura, including the routes, is given on the map on page 13. Descriptions in the explanatory text refer to these routes. For your convenience we have also turned the inner side of the back flap into a map of the area indicating all the described routes.

 shade is sparse

 suitable to walk

 suitable to drive

 beautiful scenery

 historical and cultural significance

 interesting invertebrate life

 interesting birdlife

 interesting flora

 visualising the ecological contexts described in this guide

Table of contents

LANDSCAPE

Extremadura

Like Paradise. That is the shortest description of Extremadura in spring. Old, majestic oaks dotting a rolling green tapestry of pasture. Little lambs frolicking through endless orchards, their mother standing knee-deep in a sea of wildflowers. In the pools, happy brown pigs are up to their bellies in mud. Little ribbons of white flowers dangle from their snouts. A stork soars down to its nest on the roof of an old church, where it is greeted by its partner and the rest of the stork community, numbering over fifteen nests. Welcome to Extremadura.

Extremadura is a remote region in southwestern Spain, bordering Portugal. Its rugged and infertile soil kept the Extremadura on the periphery of civilisation. For a long time, it was scorned by the Spanish and disregarded by the rest of the world. But this attitude has taken a 180-degree turn since eco-tourism became in vogue. And with good reason, for the region has great things in store for all sorts of travellers.
If birdwatching is your thing, Extremadura offers you skies filled with eagles and vultures, and steppes alive with little and great bustards. If you love to search for beautiful wildflowers, the sheer diversity of Mediterranean bulbs and orchids will dazzle you, especially in the mountains. In the endless orchards and along flower-fringed streams you'll find yourself in the Garden of Eden, while nearby rocky mountain slopes and merciless semi-deserts show a beauty of a much more rugged nature. Remote, regions invite you for a hike, and in the evening you can quietly enjoy a wonderful meal in an old plaza while watching the geckos hunt around the streetlights attached to medieval houses and palaces.
Extremadura is a rollercoaster for every nature enthusiast, not only astonishing in its diversity but also in its genesis. If you have come to see a wilderness without a trace of human influence, you have chosen the

Holm oak dehesa at the base of the Villuercas mountains.

Extremadura, what's in a name?

If you read the introduction on the previous page it is hard to believe that 'Extremadura' is Spanish for 'extremely harsh'. While the name brings to mind harsh images
of cracked clay and barren mountains, we spoke of green pastures and rolling hills.
People unfamiliar with the region but familiar with the meaning of its name are
often utterly surprised when they see the green side of the area. Expecting to enter
a desert, they stumbled upon an oasis instead.
The origin of the name 'Extremadura' is unknown, but it is unlikely that it refers
to the harsh climate. The low-lying region is strongly influenced by the Atlantic
Ocean, and is thus more humid than many other parts in central and eastern
Spain. The unfriendly name is more likely a reference to the soil, which is acidic
and poor in nutrients: bad conditions for agriculture. The soil implies a hard life
in the country. The name might refer to those conditions.
But then again, it might refer to something entirely different. 'Extremadura' might
not mean 'extremely hard' at all. Another reading is that the name 'Extremadura'
is a corruption of 'Extremo Duero', meaning the extreme (or other side) of the
Duero, a river north of Extremadura.
Currently, this is the most accepted explanation of the word. Shepherds came from
the north and took the sheep to 'los extremos del Duero', the other side of the River
Duero, to find pasture in the winter, when in the north all was withered and frozen.

wrong spot. The majority of Extremadura's valuable natural areas evolved
through the interaction between the land and its workers. This makes the
region into a must-see example of the way nature and culture can enhance
each other.

This nature guide will introduce you to the natural splendours of this
beautiful region, explain the mechanisms behind them, and direct you to
the best places to witness it all for yourself.

Geographical overview

Extremadura is an autonomous region in southwestern Spain. To the
south, Extremadura gives way to the sparsely populated Sierra Morena of
Andalusia. The northern border coincides with the high-altitude mountains of the Sistema Central, a large mountain range that effectively cuts

The Extremaduran landscape is often compared with an African savannah.

the country in two. The Sistema Central is often referred to as 'the back-bone of Spain'. North of those mountains lies the huge upland region of Castilla-Leon. Towards the east Extremadura is bordered by the mountains of the Sierra de Guadalupe - Sierra de Toledo range.

Extremadura is a large region of 41,602 km2, roughly the size of Switzerland. It is, with little over one million inhabitants, only sparsely populated. Nevertheless, one could qualify Extremadura as an urban society. Nearly all extremeños, as the residents of Extremadura are called, live in very compact villages and towns, leaving large regions of so-called despoblados (meaning both 'uninhabited' and 'deserted region'). Villages can be over 30 kilometres apart. The in-between areas take the form of empty steppes, vast dehesas and rough mountain ranges (dehesas are a sort of savannah or orchard that we will describe extensively on page 25 and further on).

Extremadura consists of two provinces: Badajóz in the south and Cáceres in the north. Almost the entire region has large areas with great natural beauty. So much, in fact, that the vastness of the landscape might over-whelm the first-time visitor.

For this reason, we decided not to make a guide that sends you off to all the remote corners of the region. Instead, we narrowed the area down to what we believe are the most beautiful areas with the most special flora and fauna. In total we describe 6 regions in detail: Monfragüe Natural Park, Plains and dehesas of Monfragüe and Cáceres, La Vera and Valle de Jerte, Sierra de las Villuercas and La Serena.

The beating heart of Extremadura (from a naturalist's point of view) is Monfragüe Natural Park (routes 1, 2, 3 and 4) between the towns of Plasencia, Cáceres and Trujillo. Monfragüe is also labelled a 'biosphere reserve'. It comprises a small and rocky mountain range along the Tagus river. The village just south of the reserve, Torrejón el Rubio, has always been the most likely point of departure for a visit to Monfragüe, but recently the picturesque hamlet of Villarreal de San Carlos has opened some rural lodges as well. Villarreal is the only dwelling within the natural park.

Monfragüe lies like a rocky island in a sea of Mediterranean holm oak dehesa. The dehesas stretch out in all directions for kilometres on end (routes 1 and 4 to 6). Towards the north they merge with the foothills of the Sistema Central. This region is known as La Vera (routes 17 and 18). Lovely little villages and dense forests of Pyrenean oak cover the mountains.

Towards the southeast the dehesas give way to the Sierra de Villuercas (routes 15 and 16), another mountainscape, larger and more rugged than Monfragüe.

Towards the south and west the lovely holm oak orchards gradually give way to the emptiness of the steppes, which seem featureless at first glance. These plains are known as the Llanos de Cáceres, and they are famous for their healthy population of steppe birds (routes 8 to 10). It is just one of several major steppe reserves in Extremadura. The largest and most lively one is La Serena (routes 12 to 14) in the far eastern corner of Badajóz Province. La Serena is considered to be the most important region in Europe for steppe birds.

In the immediately following pages you'll find more detailed descriptions of these regions.

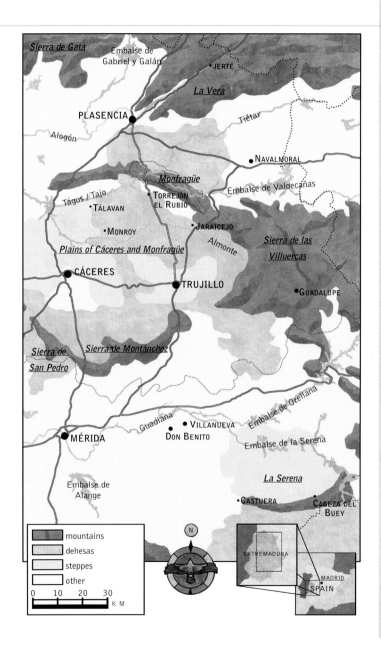

Sierra de Gata
Embalse de
Gabriel y Galán
JERTE
La Vera
PLASENCIA
Tiétar
Alogón
NAVALMORAL
Monfragüe
Embalse de Valdecañas
Tagus / Tajo
TORREJÓN
EL RUBIO
TÁLAVAN
JARAICEJO
MONROY
Almonte
Sierra de las
Villuercas
Plains of Cáceres and Monfragüe
CÁCERES
TRUJILLO
GUADALUPE
Sierra de
San Pedro
Sierra de Montánchez
Embalse de Orellana
Guadiana
VILLANUEVA
DON BENITO
MÉRIDA
Embalse de la Serena
La Serena
Embalse de
Alange
CASTUERA
CABEZA DEL
BUEY

mountains
dehesas
steppes
other
0   10   20   30
K M

N

EXTREMADURA

MADRID
SPAIN

Overview of the part
of Extremadura
described in this
guidebook.

LANDSCAPE

14

Monfragüe Natural Park

Routes 1, 2, 3 and 4 lead through Monfragüe natural park.

Monfragüe is without doubt the flagship of natural Extremadura. If this is your first visit to Extremadura, it should be your first and prime destination. This nature reserve and the surrounding land of superb cork and holm oak dehesas set a standard to which the other areas in Extremadura are best compared. Apart from the supreme wildlife and scenery, it is also the birthplace of Extremaduran nature conservation and nature tourism (see conservation and threats chapter on page 79).

Monfragüe is a natural reserve founded in 1979; in 2003 the title 'biosphere reserve' was added. It also has aspirations of becoming a national park, thereby receiving the highest protective status, which it certainly deserves.

The reserve encompasses a series of low, rocky hills along the Tagus River (*Tajo* in Spanish), with a remnant of superb dense Mediterranean forest on its north-facing slopes. The inaccessibility of the terrain has kept this area in a pristine state that you will have a hard time finding elsewhere in the present-day Mediterranean. The forest consists of nearly impene-

The Peñafalcon or vulture rock is one of the most impressive spots of Monfragüe. Over fifty pairs of griffon vultures breed on the cliff.

15

The griffon vulture is the most common raptor of Monfragüe natural park.

trable tangles of oak and many species of shrubs with a tree-like character (see chapter on Mediterranean evergreen forest on page 56). The climate underneath the canopy is surprisingly humid.

Monfragüe's fame lies mostly in its incredible number of birds of prey, which surpasses any other area in Europe. They are drawn to the park because of the generous supply of quiet and remote nesting facilities for both rock and tree nesting species, and because of the abundance of prey in the surrounding dehesas and steppes. Short-toed, booted, Bonelli's, golden and Spanish imperial eagles all breed in the roughly 10 by 30 kilometre area and can be observed anywhere in and around Monfragüe. No less than 11 pairs of Spanish imperial eagles breed in the park, which is tremendous considering that this eagle is among the most endangered in the world. There are only about 170 pairs left. Yet the grand prize goes to the vultures, which breed in astonishing numbers in the park. Around 450 pairs of griffon vultures occur in scattered colonies on cliffs all over the park, and some of them can be observed with great ease. Black vultures breed mainly on old cork oaks throughout the park. With 257 pairs, it is the largest population in Europe and possibly in the world. Other important populations of breeding birds include Egyptian vultures, peregrine falcons, eagle owls and black storks.

Much of the park is off-limits to visitors, but the sites and trails that are open to the public simply must not be missed on any trip to Extremadura.

The limited access to the park and the attractive wildlife make Monfragüe rather crowded with tourists. Especially in spring, when the tourist season is at its peak, this can spoil the fun a little. But what Monfragüe may lack in terms of tranquillity is made up for by the endless plains and the larger and more remote mountain ranges in Extremadura.

The Lange's orchid is just one of the beautiful wildflowers in the Mediterranean evergreen forest.

LANDSCAPE

Plains and dehesas of Cáceres and Monfragüe

Routes 5 to 11 lead through the steppes and dehesas of the plains around Cáceres and south of Monfragüe.

The plains between Cáceres and Trujillo are not a well-defined area, but extend north beyond the low mountain range of Monfragüe and south to the Sierra de Montánchez. To the east by the Villuercas mountains and to the west there is no clear geographical border. In this large region lie the cities of Cáceres and Trujillo and several villages, such as Torrejón el Rubio, Monroy, Serradilla, Talaván, Jaraicejo, Belén and Santa Marta de Magasca.

This large area is the true face of Extremadura: a large region of rolling steppes and holm oak dehesas that rank amongst the top in Europe. The landscape continuously and almost unnoticeably changes from very lovely and flowery to harsh and rugged. Either way, it is very scenic.

The dehesas are a sort of very extensive orchard (see chapter on dehesas on page 25 for more details), where flocks of sheep, cows and pigs graze in the pasture beneath the trees. The dehesa landscape is vast but very diverse and is home to many reptiles and insects. Many birds prey on them, such as hoopoes, woodchat and southern grey shrikes, bee-eaters, azure-winged magpies and little owls. They breed here in exceptional densities. In winter, thousands of cranes alight the dehesas to feed on the acorns.

Extensive, flowery grasslands dominate the landscape between Cáceres and Trujillo.

The steppes have a similarly rich wildlife, full of bustards, sandgrouse, stone curlews and other birds of arid landscapes. The plains are also the hunting grounds for the many vultures and eagles that breed in the mountains and remote parts of the dehesas.

The undulating land is carved by sudden steep-sloped and rocky river valleys. Next to a few rivers, with streaming water during most of the year, Extremadura has countless *arroyos*: creeks that only carry water during the rainy season and afterwards turn into a string of desiccating ponds. The amphibian life in both rivers and creeks is very rich and the springtime ribbons of white-flowering water-crowfoot are an unforgettable sight.

Cork oaks are used for the production of cork, which is peeled off the trunk in the summer months.

Champagne's orchids grow in moist spots in the dehesas.

The plains are very sparsely populated. Small villages are like little dots in the landscape and lie tens of kilometres apart. In between there is hardly a human structure to be found, except for the occasional large farm. Yet neither steppes nor dehesas are natural landscapes. Instead they came into being through centuries of traditional and nature-friendly landuse. The land is mostly in private hands and is divided into large *fincas*, estates, that can measure up to 4,000 hectares. Estates of less than 100 hectares are a rarity.

This makes the dehesas and steppes a difficult area to visit. Free passage is mostly impossible, but there are some freely accessible tracks, and river valleys are in principle public land.

La Vera and the Jerte valley

> Routes 17 and 18 are a good introduction to the mountains of La Vera and the Jerte valley. Within the area there are many other hiking options, which we mention on page 179.

The Sistema Central is a large mountain chain that divides the Iberian Peninsula into two. It does not reach the altitudes of the Pyrenees or the Sierra Nevada, but with peaks of up to 2592 m (Mount Almanzor) it ranks most definitely amongst the Alpine mountains and is snow-covered well into the summer.

Hillside above Garganta la Olla (route 17). Young Pyrenean oaks now grow where once were scrublands and chestnut groves.

La Vera is a part of the southern slopes of the Sistema Central and the northern part of Extremadura. It is a beautiful region with lush, green slopes clad with Pyrenean oak forests and cherry and chestnut groves. Numerous fresh mountain streams thunder down into the dehesas of the plains. One of the larger ones is the Jerte River, which cuts a deep valley from Tornavacas on the northern edge of Extremadura to the town of Plasencia at the base of the mountains.

In contrast to central European mountains, the high slopes of La Vera and Jerte Valley are not characterised by flowery meadows, but by a low scrubland of bushes, consisting mostly of heaths, brooms and gorses.

Although the mountains of La Vera and the Jerte Valley are close to Monfragüe and the surrounding lowlands, they form an entirely different world. To the visitor they offer a perfect opportunity for beautiful walks and for getting a taste of a different culture and friendly people.

Compared to the lowland, the wildlife of La Vera is less dominated by birds. Many of the Mediterranean bird species have been replaced with central European ones. However, the region houses a much more diverse flora and a wide variety of butterflies, reptiles and mammals.

Shrubby gromwell (top) and early purple orchid (bottom), two plants that do well in the acidic soil of the mountains.

Sierra de las Villuercas

Routes 15 and 16 offer a good introduction to the Sierra de las Villuercas. Within the area there are several other excursion options, which we discuss briefly on page 185.

Tucked away in the eastern part of the Cáceres province are the rugged mountains known as the Sierra de las Villuercas (pronounced: Bi-yu-ER-cas). They do not reach as high as the Sistema Central, but with a highest point of 1601 metres, they form a good mid-range.

The Villuercas mountains are one of those 'secret tips' for visitors. It would probably be one of the most unknown regions of Extremadura, were it not for the picturesque town of Guadalupe located in the heart of

Autumn colours in the Sierra de las Villuercas.

the mountain chain. With its beautiful monastery and the famous 'Virgen de Guadalupe', the second most important shrine of the Holy Virgin in Spain, Guadalupe attracts a fair number of pilgrims from all over Europe. The hills and mountains around Guadalupe are a paradise for those seeking tranquillity, good hiking trails, splendid scenery and a rich flora and fauna.

The mountains hold somewhat of a middle position between the mountains of the Sistema Central (La Vera) and of Monfragüe (which is in fact the western continuation of the Villuercas). They are high enough to support the mountain forests of Pyrenean oak, chestnut groves and Atlantic heathland, but they

Monastery of Guadalupe

also have, like Monfragüe, those rocky outcrops overlooking the valley, which makes the Villuercas equally attractive to breeding raptors.

Unique to the Villuercas is its vegetation, a relict from the Tertiary period, an era during which Europe had a much more humid, sub-tropical climate. The plants of those ages largely disappeared with the birth of the Mediterranean climate, but some lingered on in moister areas, such as the valleys of las Villuercas.

Cherry tree in flower near Navazuelas (route 15).

La Serena

Routes 12, 13 and 14 lead you through the steppes of La Serena and nearby mountains.

On the very eastern edge of Extremadura, in the province of Badajóz, lies a region with a landscape that seems made for cowboys and car commercials. It consists of endless, rolling hills, covered with tawny pasture, the occasional scruffy shrub and groups of rocks with an odd, tombstone-like appearance. High overhead, the silhouette of a griffon vulture stands out against a bright blue sky. In the background you see the rocky skyline of some nameless sierra.

The occasional ruin and farm in La Serena accentuate the emptiness of the plains.

This is la Serena, the apotheosis of the romance of emptiness. It is virtually treeless, save the occasional large eucalyptus tree along the few roads that traverse the area.

The romance of la Serena appears in its indifferent and featureless landscape. But this is deceiving. It is not an anonymous region at all, but famous for its unsurpassed arid grassland birdlife. It is of tremendous importance as a refuge for great and little bustards, black-bellied and pin-

tailed sandgrouse and stone curlews, which occur by the thousands under a sky that is pregnant with singing calandra larks.
The ecological importance of the area lies in the fact that it has many different types of steppes, from the most scanty terrain full of pointy 'dog-teeth' rocks to extensive open grasslands, cereal fields and ploughed land (see steppes section on page 48).
Villages around the plains are situated in a half circle at the foot of a rugged mountain range, the Sierra de Tiros. This mountain range is to la Serena what Monfragüe is to the plains of Cáceres and Trujillo: the breeding place of eagles and vultures that hunt in the steppes. The rocky outcrops harbour a plant and wildlife that offers a day's worth of examination as well.

Crested lark (top) and the similar Thekla lark are both numerous in la Serena. Spanish sparrows (bottom) live in groups in the large Eucalyptus trees along some of the minor roads. Despite its name, it is a rare bird in Spain, only numerous in central Extremadura. Spanish sparrows are more common in southeastern Europe.

24

Habitats

Oscar Wilde once said, "The true mystery of the world is the visible, not the invisible." Unravelling this mystery, or trying to do so, is a fascinating pastime, to say the least. To get anywhere near an understanding of the visible natural world -in this case of the Extremadura region- you will need a concept as a framework into which you can place what you see around you. For a biologist such a concept is that of a 'habitat'.

A habitat is best defined as a tight interaction between plants, animals, soil and climate in a given area. The latter two form a landscape where a specific set of plants and animals feel at home. Habitats are the cornerstone of the way a biologist looks at a landscape and understands it. It is an extremely useful tool, not only for experts, but also for first-time visitors. Without this tool the occurrence of plants and animals seems a matter of chance, and the presence of patterns and structures in the landscape remains unexplained or even unnoticed. But if you look at a landscape in terms of habitats you will get an understanding of that landscape and of the challenges, curses and blessings it brings to its inhabitants. The behaviour of birds, the shape of flowers, the colour of leaves and even the smell of the landscape can be understood when seen in the context of habi-

Schematic cross-section of Extremadura from the mountains of La Vera in the north (routes 17, 18) down to the dehesas and steppes between Cáceres and Trujillo (routes 8 - 10). This cross-section shows all major habitats of Extremadura, which are described on the following pages.

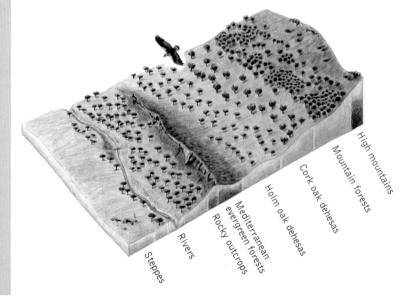

tats and habitat adaptations. Of course this brings up a truckload of new questions. The fascinating thing about unravelling Oscar Wilde's mystery is that it makes a lot more visible. That is, it enables you to find plants and animals and to discover principles and processes that would otherwise have remained hidden to you.

With all of this in mind, this guidebook has been organised around the habitats of Extremadura. The routes we suggest to you have been carefully chosen to give the best possible introduction to all the habitats in the region, thereby optimising your chances of seeing all the plants and animals.

Dehesa

The dehesa is the most dominant landscape type in Extremadura and therefore forms an important element in almost every trip. A large part of the whole lowland region north of Trujillo and Cáceres is covered by dehesa. The oldest, richest and most beautiful stands are found along routes 1, 2, 8 and 15.

Pick any road or track around the Monfragüe nature reserve. Go from Torrejón to Serradilla. Or Monroy. Or Jaraicejo. Stop anywhere along the road and take in the scenery. Look over the fence towards the gradually tree-blocked horizon. What is behind it is anyone's guess, but closer by, the image is clearer. Gnarled oak stems curl out from behind pointed rocks, fringed with foxglove and asphodel tufts. Above the gentle breeze you hear hoopoes calling and Thekla larks singing from several directions. Five griffon vultures glide over, directly followed by a short-toed eagle and an Egyptian vulture.

This is not an exaggeration, but a real image of the dehesas of Extremadura in spring: a paradise for nature enthusiasts.

What are dehesas?

The rolling, tree-dotted hills and plains of Extremadura are called dehesas. They undoubtedly form the most typical and most unique landscape of Extremadura.

That being said, the dehesa landscape is hard to define. There are no good comparisons with better known landscapes that really catch the essence of the dehesa. Sometimes dehesas are called Mediterranean forests, but that is not quite right. There are but few dehesas that are so densely covered with trees that they really resemble a forest.

The aesthetic correctness of the dehesa

For the sake of nature conservation, the nature of Extremadura has been extensively researched. But the investigations have concerned more than nature alone. Believe it or not, you have been put under the microscope as well -and the results are interesting indeed.

The aesthetic perception of landscapes has become a considerable subject of psychological research. If you are in for some psychology, the results make for a great read, because they hold up a mirror to all nature enthusiasts. The research identifies which landscapes are generally considered beautiful and attempts to explain the underlying reasons.

In this context the dehesa not only entered the beauty pageant, but more or less became Miss Landscape. Environmental psychologists have studied people's perception of landscapes and discovered that the dehesas are aesthetically 'perfectly correct'. They exhibit many aspects of the ideal, pastoral landscape and score high for four reasons: their visual depth, their naturalness, their moderate complexity and the presence of water.

Depth in a landscape is a proven winner. With a little something in the foreground and trees gradually receding into the background, the dehesas provide a lot of depth. In numerous tests, research participants have been shown a variety of open and closed landscapes, ranging from endless flat fields to dense walls of vegetation. The in-between version, with a cosy foreground and a good view into the distance, invariably came out first.

The naturalness of the landscape is a very interesting factor in aesthetic appreciation. Natural landscapes are perceived as more beautiful than man-made landscapes, regardless of whether they really are natural or not. In several research projects, respondents have been asked to rate natural and planted forest landscapes on the basis of a number of photographs. They were informed in advance about the type of landscape shown to them. Almost invariably, the natural ones were much more highly valued. A next group of participants was asked the same question, only this time the managed forest was said to be natural and the natural said to be managed (one of the psychologist's nasty tricks). This time the group preferred the managed forest (the one they thought was natural). This test shows that it is much more the idea of naturalness than naturalness itself that influences nature appreciation. Dehesas appear to be natural, even though they are in fact an agricultural landscape.

Another factor influencing appreciation is complexity. A landscape shouldn't be so complex that it is difficult to grasp visually, but also not so empty that it becomes boring.

Beautiful landscapes are often mistaken for the most ecologically valuable. And therein lies the problem that makes the psychological journey into landscape aes-

thetics so interesting: is nature conservation a question of preserving the most beautiful nature or preserving the nature that is most ecologically valuable? Or do these two coincide?

The first nature reserves protected wild and dramatic landscapes, featuring sheer cliffs, exciting wildlife and bursting waterfalls. The advocates of nature conservation could therefore count on a broad public support. But when conservation became more technical and started to focus on more mundane landscapes with high ecological values, things started to get more difficult. Suddenly the link between the beautiful and the ecologically valuable was less evident. Thus it became an interesting problem whether such a link really exists.

The most beautiful dehesas are those with a good depth of vision, a natural appearance and some flowers in the foreground -in this case Spanish white broom.

Fortunately, the outcome of the research has not shown an evident clash between the two approaches. Water-rich areas are often of great importance for nature as well as for creating beautiful landscapes. Structure-rich landscapes offer homes to many plants and animals. Landscapes that appear natural or harmonious are usually rich in species. And so on.

On the other hand, landscape aesthetics doesn't have all the answers. There are so many other reasons why landscapes can be beautiful and many of them are very personal or specific to a certain group of people.

So, getting back to you again, there is nothing wrong with you if you like empty, ploughed fields from here to the horizon and if dehesas are not your thing. But then, being in Extremadura, you do have a problem...

In more scientific circles they are referred to as Mediterranean savannah, which comes closer. However, this is still not quite satisfactory, because the vast majority of dehesas are not as spacious and open as the only savannah that is familiar to all of us, the African savannah. Many dehesas are rather secluded, with a more lush and colourful vegetation than their African counterparts. We think dehesas are better compared with orchards. If asked for a one-sentence definition of a dehesa, we would say that it is a giant, never-ending grove of trees with pasture and crops underneath.

Dehesas in Extremadura consist predominantly of holm oak, which is replaced by cork oak on the richer, more humid soils at the base of the mountains. Occasionally, you can also encounter dehesas consisting of Lusitanian and Pyrenean oaks and, more rarely, narrow-leaved ash as well. Extremadura and dehesas go together like horses and carrots. The 'orchards' cover little over 50% of the land of Extremadura, but are rare outside the region except for in adjacent Andalusia and Portugal. Extremadura holds about 50% of the world's dehesas and is therefore called the 'heartland' of the dehesa. Outside the Iberian Peninsula dehesas are nearly non-existent, so they form a unique landscape indeed.

Around 50% of the land of Extremadura is covered by dehesas.

The holm oak is the most common dehesa tree.

The perfect man-nature hybrid

Although dehesas boast a tremendous flora and fauna (we will rave about this a little further on), they are not a natural landscape in the sense of being free of human influence. On the contrary, dehesas are a man-made landscape: moulded, modelled, reshaped and touched up over centuries of hard country life.

The first evidence of human meddling with the original vegetation dates back to about 4,000 years ago. The pristine Mediterranean forest -a habitat that is now pretty much extinct, except for in Monfragüe (routes 1, 2, 3 and 4)- was thinned and the dense undergrowth was burned to create pasture for grazing cattle (see history section on page 70 and text box on page 60).

The change from forest to dehesa happened slowly and a long time ago. Since then, changes have been relatively minor. Of course the dehesa has seen many shifts in landowner regime, increases and decreases in live-stock densities and so on, but these hardly compare to the transition agri-culture made in central Europe. The Extremaduran soil simply cannot support intensive agriculture -it is too thin. (Although socio-economic changes in the second half of the 20th century did change the face of the dehesa; see page 78 to 81).

As a result, management of the dehesas leaves a prominent role to natural processes. During the gradual conversion into dehesa, nature was able to develop according to the changes in the landscape, adapting itself to new lifestyles, with species that exist in harmony with traditional human practise. Today, the dehesas support a number of very rare and endangered animals, such as the Spanish imperial eagle and black vulture, as well as numerous others that are becoming increasingly rare in other areas in Europe.

A unique form of landuse

One hardly ever notices it, but a really traditional approach to land use has silently disappeared from the scene of Europe's countryside: agro-forestry, the marriage of forest and farmer, animal and acorn, cattle and coppice.

Today, except in a few nature reserves, forestry is strictly separated from husbandry. Forestry takes place in plantations and forests, husbandry on the pastures. But this was not always the case. In the middle ages cattle often grazed in open, park-like forests. The German word *Hudewald* translates into 'tending-forest' and refers to a forest that was used to feed cattle and to provide fodder, firewood and timber. In the New Forest in southern England the locals, known as the commoners, were allowed to let their ponies, donkeys and pigs graze in the open forest. The timber was reserved for the Crown. These forests look quite a bit like dehesas, with grasslands between groups of trees and bushes.

Indeed, dehesas also provide both pasture for grazing cattle and timber products such as cork, firewood, acorns and charcoal (see text box on page 38). The Extremaduran dehesas are a fine specimen of the open-air museum of agricultural practice, forming one of the last agro-forestry systems that is still up and running.

But there is more to it. Strictly speaking, the dehesas are an agro-sylvo-pastoral landscape. They involve a third form of land use: the growing of cereal crops. As such, the dehesa is one of a kind, the only landscape in Europe that combines three forms of land use in one space. The significance to nature of this triple-land-use agriculture is shown in the figure on page 32.

Thus, even if stripped of its scenic value and its rich flora and fauna, the dehesa would remain of interest for its unique form of agriculture.

How do dehesas work?

Dehesas thrive in a climate that already favours the growth of individual trees rather than entire forests. The poor soils and lack of water inhibit rapid growth of vegetation. In the course of tens of years, a low forest can gradually establish itself, but if people selectively cut and burn the vegetation and tend grazing animals, you easily end up with pasture and solitary trees: dehesas.

The dehesa ecosystem revolves around the establishment and disappearance of pasture. If you were to photograph a single dehesa over the years, you would see it change from a loosely planted cereal field into a pasture and then into scrubland (see illustration on the following page).

Grain is sown every four to seven years. Barley, wheat and -on very poor soils- oats are the dominant crops, which are primarily used as fodder. The thin layer of soil can produce only one harvest, then it is exhausted, turned to pasture and left to recover. Sheep, cattle and pigs invade the fallow land. Via the fur and droppings of grazing sheep, plant seeds also arrive, much to the satisfaction of the farmer, who has one thing less to worry about. The wind also lends a hand in the spreading of plant seeds.

Winter image of an old cork oak dehesa.

Dehesa with cereal cultivation

The cycle of the dehesa

Dehesas are used for cereal cultivation (top left). After one year of growing cereal the soil is exhausted and left to recover. It turns into pasture (top right) for sheep and cattle. In the course of the follow-ing years the dehesa is invaded with low scrub (bottom right) that gradually makes way for higher scrub-land (bottom left). This is removed and the plot is planted with cereal again.

Depending on the fertility of the soil the dehesa cycle takes between four and seven years to complete.

Dehesa with scrubland

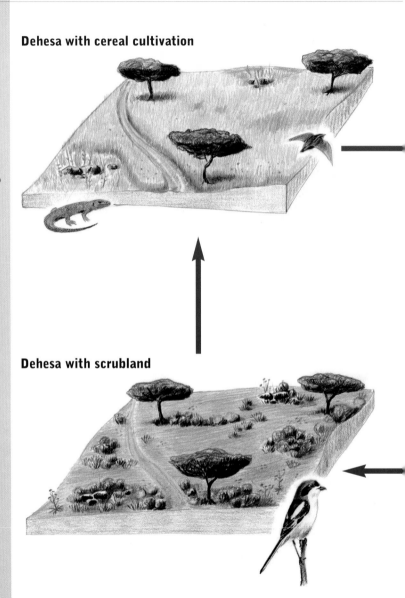

Dehesa with pasture

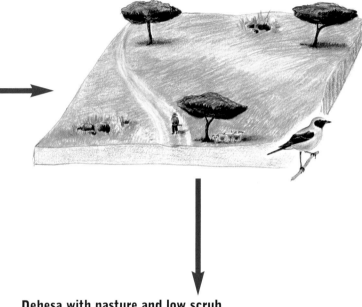

Nature and the dehesa cycle

Each stage in the cycle supports its own particular flora and fauna. This is what makes the dehesa unique: the display of four different habitats in a single area. Because the rocks and tree canopies remain intact throughout the cycle, they function as a refuge for plants and animals for the periods the dehesa doesn't meet their requirements.

Dehesa with pasture and low scrub

But the livestock does not only bring grasses and edible herbs with them. French lavender, wild thyme, white asphodel, Lusitanian milkvetch, spiny greenweed* and sage-leaved and gum cistusses invade the pasture. And of course holm and cork oaks germinate from the plentiful acorns. Gradually the dehesa starts to become trees-over-scrub instead of trees-over-pasture, until the farmer intervenes. He cuts or burns the entire undergrowth, ploughs the ground and sows grain anew.

Thus, the dehesa shows a continuously shifting pattern of different stages of fallow land, pasture, scrubland and grain fields, each with its own set of plants and animals. The fallow land attracts seed-eating birds, the grassy dehesas host large insects and their predators, and the scrublands give shelter to wild boars, lizards and snakes and perches to woodchat shrikes and Dartford warblers.

Now, if you adopt a bird's eye view to examine the dehesa landscape as a whole, instead of a single plot, you see a pattern of shifting cultivation. The dehesa landscape shows a continuously changing pattern of fields, pastures and scrublands underneath the open canopy of evergreen oaks. Every plot of dehesa is in a different stage in this cycle. The dehesas over poor soils take six or seven years to complete, whilst the more fertile ones are back to barley again within three to four years.

The flora and fauna docilely move along with the turning of the wheel, searching out the plots with the undergrowth that best suits their needs. In this continuously changing system, the trees, rocks and pool sides form a steady factor. They are non-ploughable little corners and play a key role in the ecology of the dehesa. They remain grassy and shrubby patches regardless of the state of the surrounding dehesa. During the more unfavourable periods of the dehesa life cycle, these spots function as a refuge for smaller and less mobile animals, such as lizards and insects.

Wildlife of the dehesa

The result of this joint enterprise between man and nature is impressive, to say the least. Apart from the splendid scenery, the flora and fauna of the dehesas are extremely rich. A famous Spanish research project in 1985 showed that the plant life reaches up to 45 species per square metre! This is an extraordinarily high number that immediately drew attention to the dehesas of Extremadura, which up until then were largely neglected.

Despite these statistics, the dehesas are not a great hotspot for botanists. Most of these species are short-living grasses and crucifers that occur throughout the dehesa and a fair portion of the Mediterranean basin. More interesting are the damper pastures in the little valleys. Provided

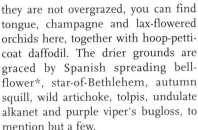

they are not overgrazed, you can find tongue, champagne and lax-flowered orchids here, together with hoop-petti-coat daffodil. The drier grounds are graced by Spanish spreading bell-flower*, star-of-Bethlehem, autumn squill, wild artichoke, tolpis, undulate alkanet and purple viper's bugloss, to mention but a few.

The birdlife in the dehesas of Extrema-dura is nothing short of phenomenal and draws birdwatchers from all over Europe. The dehesa birdlife is richer than that of the steppes and also out-ranks that of the Mediterranean evergreen forest. Within the dehe-sas, species proper to steppes, for-est, small-scale agriculture land and scrublands meet, creating a hodgepodge of birds.

Forest birds are represented by several well-known species, such as the chaffinch, song thrush, blackbird and great spotted wood-pecker. These species are most numerous in the denser dehesas and reside in the thick canopy of the trees. The birds of small-scale agri-cultural land are comprised of hoopoes, bee-eaters, azure-winged magpies, little owls, serins, corn buntings, goldfinch-es and wood larks. The dehesas with fewer trees draw to the steppes. Thekla larks, stone curlews, little bustards and southern grey shrikes enjoy these parts. Dehesas with lots of shrubby under-growth attract Mediterranean scrub-land species, such as Sardinian and Dartford warblers and woodchat shrikes.

The barbary nut (top), a species of iris, grows in dry, often somewhat trampled parts of the dehesas. The Lusitanian spreading bellflower* (middle) prefers the less grazed pastures.

Of all the birds that live in the dehesas, the azure-winged magpie (bottom) is most tied to this par-ticular habitat.

But the raptors take the cake. They hunt the dehesas and steppes in exceptional numbers. Some of them breed in the dehesas, others in the
Mediterranean forests and rocky Sierras that cut through Extremadura,
but they all rely on the plains for their food. It is the carcasses of animals
they are after. Sheep, cows, pigs, and goats easily get lost in the rugged,
endless terrain. The combination of a juicy twig, an unstable escarpment
and a ravine will do the trick. An unfortunate rest on a scorpion's den or
simply old age or a disease will do as well. While there are countless ways
to leave this world, animal flesh in Extremadura has but one: through the
stomach of a vulture.

Griffon vultures are especially numerous, but the black vulture -rare on a
global scale- is present in good numbers as well. Smaller birds of prey,
such as Egyptian vultures, black and red kites, and golden and Spanish
imperial eagles get their share whenever they can, as do foxes.

Scarabs and other insects also live off these dead animals and form an
important food source for the birds that live off large insects (bee-eaters,
hoopoes, woodchat shrikes, great spotted cuckoos et cetera). As such, husbandry is firmly linked with the natural side of the dehesa.

In this respect, the agriculture hygiene frenzy of the European Union's
agriculture policies is a potential hazard to the dehesas. New laws dictate
that corpses of deceased animals have to be cleaned up, leaving the vultures without food. Luckily, the paper reality drawn up from behind a desk
in Brussels is no match for the reality of the field. Sheep in the dehesa
fend for themselves throughout most of the year and the terrain is simply

This dead cow is com-
pletely devoured by
vultures. Only the
bones and the skin
remain, now dry and
hard from the merci-
less sun.

The large wings of vultures are perfectly adapted to use the hot, rising air. It lifts them up and keeps them in the air, so they can effortlessly scout the plains for recently deceased animals.

much too big to notice a missing sheep and go out looking for it. Besides, many of the dead animals the vultures feed on are wild animals such as red deer and wild boar.

A key element explaining the richness of the dehesas of Extremadura is the size. They are sizable enough to harbour animals with large territories. A good example is the very rare and highly endangered Spanish imperial eagle. This impressive bird hunts for rabbits and needs to cover a large terrain to feed a single family. The total surface of the dehesas is large enough to support not only this family, but also enough other pairs to make up a healthy population.

On the other hand, dehesas are, paradoxically, a small-scale landscape. And this is a positive aspect as well. Each little patch of dehesa is different. Little things like a stonewall, a shag, a group of gum cistus bushes, an old cork oak-in other words, any of the whole set of features we mentioned at the beginning of this chapter -create a nearly endless variety of little habitats in the landscape. Together they provide a living space for many different small animals and large insects, as well as offering ample nesting facilities for the animals that feed upon them. Stonewalls are full of Iberian wall lizards and Moorish geckos; their predator, the hoopoe, breeds in shags. Gum cistus bushes are residences of the Montpellier snake. It goes out hunting for the eggs of the hoopoe, but turns up as dinner for the short-toed eagles breeding in the old cork oak. And so on. The small-scale differences in the sizable dehesas are the reason for the incredible numbers of birds that eat those mid-sized animals. A day-trip through the dehesas in spring can yield tens of hoopoes, twice as many woodchat shrikes, several southern grey shrikes, hundreds of kites, several owls, tens of bee-eaters... well, you get the picture.

Products of the dehesa

In comparison to central European agriculture the dehesas are unique, because they do not yield a single crop, but produce the whole package instead: grazing ground for cattle, forestry products such as cork and charcoal, fodder, barley, honey, as well as game and birds to hunt.
Here is a short description of the festive array of products and services from the dehesa.

Pasture and grain fields: food for livestock

The prime product of the dehesa is the pasture it provides for sheep, cattle, pigs and game. The pasture is hardly comparable to central European grasslands: less green, much scantier and much less productive. The number of plant species, however, is much larger and includes several grasses, medicks, daisies and hawks-beards. Still, the extensive land of Extremadura supports a good number of graz-ers. At present, there can be up to 4 sheep per hectare, which are few in compar-ison to central Europe, but too many for the dehesas, which had an average of 1.5 sheep per hectare 60 years ago.
The pasture only provides food in the winter months. In summer the cattle is either marched off during the transhumance (text box on page 76) or fed with supple-ments, such as the fodder from the grain fields.

Trees: climate and soil regulation

The trees are not planted for the scenery. They provide a whole series of services and products. A very important service in the Mediterranean climate is that they provide shade for the animals. When hiding under the canopy, the sheep droppings add nourishment to the pasture and to the tree itself.
Another important service is slowing down erosion. Rain in Extremadura often comes in the form of a fierce deluge rather than in gentle drizzles. Without a strong canopy to block the force, the sudden plenitude of water would eat away the fertile soil and flush it down into the creeks and rivers. The broad canopies block the rain and let it through at a gentler pace. The extensive root system fixes the soil and pumps up nutrients from the underground, making them available for other plants and animals as well.
The rain may be less fierce under the canopy, but it continues for a longer period of time. Long after the sun has chased away the clouds, the water still drips from

the leaves. By spreading out the duration of the actual fall of water, trees enable the ground to take up more of it. In summer, the oak leaves filter the early morning moisture from the air. In the afternoon they effectively seal off the leaves to prevent evaporation. So all in all the trees increase the humidity and the fertility of the land.

Holm oaks play a vital role in dehesa agriculture. One of their many functions is to provide shade for cattle.

Trees: acorns, cork, fodder, wood

The holm and cork oaks also provide a product directly, namely acorns. Holm oak acorns are edible, have a sweet taste and are considered a delicacy by some. In the past, people also used them to make flour for baking bread. Today, acorns are primarily used as food for pigs.

The crowns of the oak trees are thinned in such a way that the crown becomes very broad and produces many acorns (In this shape it also performs optimally as a soil and climate regulator).

Cork oak acorns are of lesser quality, but the oak itself is in obvious demand for its cork. Cork is an ancient product, used long before it became the favourite plug for wine bottles. Its capacity to float on water was much praised. Cork was turned into floats for anglers, for fishing nets and as life-savers for children.

Cork was also converted into tiles and used as insulation for roofs and footwear. Cork oaks are larger than holm oaks and are important nesting trees for black vultures and Spanish imperial eagles. In economic terms, cork oak dehesas lean heavily upon cork production, which is an extra incentive to uncork that next bottle of wine (Acting in line with nature conservation is rarely this pleasurable).

The wood of the oaks is usually not used as timber, because their branches are too small and too gnarled. However, leaves are used as fodder and wood is used for cooking and heating.

Holm oaks are pruned to contain three or four main branches. This way they can grow the broadest canopies, which function as umbrella, parasol and acorn factory.

Livestock: pigs, sheep, goats and cattle

The Spanish love pigs. Not primarily because they are cute and intelligent, but because they are economic. There is no part of the pig that cannot be used and almost no part that cannot be eaten. Among the hams from Extremadura are the famous air-dried 'Jamón Serrano' and the prize-winning 'Jamón Ibérico'. The latter receives its taste from the acorns of the holm oak on which the pigs feed. The quality of the ham is categorised by the drying and salting process and by the time the pigs were on a diet of acorns. The Iberian ham is the most exquisite dehesa product, except maybe for the Merino wool.

Merino wool comes from Merino sheep and is praised for its outstanding quality. The history of Spain is strongly influenced by Merino sheep and their wool (see history section), but nowadays both are nearly worthless. Sheep today are kept for meat, just like cows. Goats are kept mostly for milk and to make a variety of very good goat cheeses.

Scrubland: honey and game
The flowery scrublands are the dehesas' least-valued aspect. Nevertheless, scrub is

an inevitable aspect of the dehesa and does have some important by-products. The flowers are the engine behind bee-keeping. Some of the plants are edible, such as wild artichoke, wild asparagus, mushrooms, thyme and rosemary. Moreover, scrubland is essential as a retreat for red deer, fox and wild boar -much-celebrated trophies for hunters. Many of the larger estates are owned by rich people from outside Extremadura (a major social problem in the region) and used as a pleasure hunting resort. Game, wintering thrushes and wood pigeons are plentiful in the dehesa, much to the enjoyment of the hunters. On some estates, game is the thing that matters, everything else is considered a by-product.

Latest products: nature and ecotourists
Granted, the way of putting it is debatable, but in a way you could say that the dehesas' latest products are eco- and nature tourists. The unprecedented importance to nature has given the dehesa a value beyond straightforward economic gain. Large areas are already under some form of protection.

Ecotourism, on the other hand, can be measured in economic terms. Tourism has taken a flight in recent decades and tourists bring money into the area. The awareness is growing that the scenic beauty and impressive nature, especially the birdlife, have become a source of income.

Creeks, rivers and reservoirs

Lowland creeks and rivers can be admired along routes 1, 4, 8 and 12. The Almonte river is very beautiful south of Torrejón, near Monroy and in the Villuercas mountains (route 15). Other marvellous rivers are the Viejas river (route 16) and the one running through the gorge 'Garganta de los infiernos' (route 18). Reservoirs of interest are the Embalse de la Serena (route 12) and Guadiloba (route 8) and the small ones near Talaván and Torrejón (route 7).

The many creeks and rivers are undoubtedly among Extremadura's most beautiful landscape features. After a rainy winter, spring comes with an abundance of wildflowers along the streams of Extremadura. Masses of water-crowfoot float on the water like foam on a hot bath. The trickling streams, together with the Arcadian dehesas, make the picture of Extremadura as the Garden of Eden complete. If there were a picture next to 'picturesque' in the dictionary, it ought to be one of an Extremaduran creek in spring.

River valleys are like incisions in the rolling plains of Extremadura. This is the steep river valley of Arroyo de la Vid, just north of the village of Torrejón.

Extremadura has a lot of surface water. The prevailing western winds and the region's position near the Atlantic temper the harshness of the Mediterranean climate. The air brings water from the ocean, making Extremadura a much moister region than most of central and eastern Spain. The mountains in the north (Sierra de Gata, La Vera) and east (Sierra de las Villuercas) intercept the lion's share of the rain and carry it back west through the creeks and rivers of Extremadura.

Add to this the Spanish tendency to retain every drop of freshwater and Extremadura's solid bedrock, through which hardly a drop of water penetrates, and it is no surprise that there is so much blue on the map of Extremadura.

Creeks and rivers

Aquatic environments come in four types: creeks (*arroyos*), rivers (*rios*), and two types of reservoirs (*pantanos* or *embalses*).

In contrast to rivers, creeks only have a good flow of water during and right after periods of heavy rainfall. It takes only a few weeks of sunshine to reduce the water flow to a small trickle and finally to a string of slowly desiccating pools. Nevertheless, the abundance of life in these creeks is astounding. The reptile and amphibian world catches the eye and ear the most. In spring, Perez's frogs -the Spanish version of the pool frog- croak loudly from the water during the day. At night, they are replaced by the somewhat foolish *pjuups* of the Iberian midwife toads (when you hear this call coming from a tree, you are standing under a scops owl, which has a similar call).

Apart from Perez's frogs and Iberian midwife toads, you can find common toads and sharp-ribbed salamanders. Marbled and Bosca's newts are also numerous. Stripeless treefrogs climb through the surrounding vegetation of bramble and tamujo*, a common streamside bush that is unique to southwestern Iberia. Stripe-necked terrapins love to sunbathe on a rock or log. They usually huddle together and are easy to spot, provided you proceed with care and scan the rocks with binoculars before going down to the creek. Stripe-necked terrapins are very shy and disappear into the water as soon as they notice you.

The small snakes you can find under the rocks in shallow pools are viperine snakes, harmless animals that go after small fish and tadpoles.

Unlike creeks, rivers usually keep up a good pace of water throughout the year, provided that winter brought sufficient rain. All the large rivers of Extremadura are dammed at least once. The Tagus (or *Tajo* in Spanish) is even dammed so often that it hardly qualifies as a river anymore, but has become a string of reservoirs instead. Only a few smaller ones, like the Almonte and Tozo Rivers, still run their natural course.

Natural rivers have a similar wildlife as the creeks, only more pronounced. There are more fish and there are otters to hunt them. Black storks search for amphibians on the water's edge.

Away from the riverbed, the valley is at least as interesting. Since the soil surfacing in Extremadura is very old, rivers have had ages to cut them- selves deep into the bedrock. As a result, the slopes of the river valleys are steep and overgrown with a thick and little-grazed scrubland of holm oak. These slopes are perfect to search for the rarer plants of the dehesas, such as milky orchid, snakeshead and Spanish iris. Near the river there are moist, grassy patches where the river only floods when water levels are high. These patches are interesting for their wildflowers, which include several orchids too, like tongue, champagne, lax-flowered and bug orchids.

The river valleys in lowland Extremadura are like inversions of its moun- tain ranges. They are just as steep and usually just as rocky. Only instead of rising up, the surface dives down. With this in mind it is not surprising that the bird community in river valleys is rather similar to that of, for example, Monfragüe. In the valleys of the Almonte and the Arroyo de la Vid (just north of Torrejón el Rubio) and in El Cabril (south of Monroy) breed eagle owls, short-toed eagles, black storks, Egyptian vultures, blue rock thrushes, rock sparrows, rock buntings, crag martins, red-rumped swallows, and so on. They are all breeding birds proper to rocky places and also breed in Monfragüe.

The large sharp- ribbed salamander, unique to the Iberian Peninsula, is perfectly adapted to life in the temporary pools and streams.

Along the river margins you can find kingfishers, Spanish sparrows, little ringed plovers, pied wagtails and common sandpipers. All in all, the rivers and creeks are true bird hotspots, much unlike the region's reservoirs.

Stripe-necked terrapins galore in Extremadura.

Reservoirs

Extremadura's largest rivers are the Tiétar, the Tagus and the Guadiana. The Tiétar has only one dam, but the other two have been dammed several times. The dams were built in the 1960s to create huge water reservoirs, like the Embalses de Alcántara, Embalse de Valdecaños and Embalse de La Serena. The creeks and small rivers are usually dammed at some point as well, to create small reservoirs for the water supply of the villages.

The natural value of the large and small reservoirs differs considerably. The main purpose of the large ones is to generate electricity. To build up sufficient water pressure to produce electricity, you need to seek out a location with steep slopes. Thus the large reservoirs are found along the large rivers in deeply creviced terrain. As a result, there is not much of a shoreline. The unpredictable water level fluctuations in the reservoir kill off the vegetation in a large zone. In winter you might find the occasional cormorant and grey heron around the reservoir, but that is it.

The story on the small reservoirs is a lot less gloomy. They are often found in more gently rolling terrain, giving the lake something of a shoreline with a little reed, larger herbs, and thus some waterfowl. A few reservoirs have developed small marshlands in the margins, such as the one near

Almaráz (route 1). Here you can find some nice birds you wouldn't exactly associate with Extremadura, like great reed warblers, Savi's warblers, little bitterns, purple herons and, recently, purple gallinules.

Some of the reservoirs take up an enormous surface and form a spectacular clean landscape. Unfortunately, there is not much life in them.

Creeks in the mountains

Creeks in the mountains create a unique microclimate. To experience this you ought to descend a south slope to the stream at the bottom of the valley. The valley of the river Viejas (Route 16) in the Villuercas Mountains is perfect in this respect. As soon as you reach the bottom of the narrow valley you can feel the atmosphere change. The temperature drops considerably and the atmosphere becomes moist. The river valley is secluded and shaded by a thick canopy that the keeps the dampness in and the sunlight out. The murmuring creek produces a constant spray of fine droplets, which keeps the temperature and humidity at a rather constant level. During the morning, the cool water surface captures the moisture of the air, creating a cool mist. All these factors contribute to the establishment of a unique 'moisture bubble' along the course of the river.

There are a few plants and animals that can only survive in this refuge of dampness and coolness. The surrounding terrain is too dry and too hot. The most special plant is the Portuguese laurel (p. 87), a small tree that grows directly alongside the water. It is a relict from the cloud forests of the Tertiary period, which once covered a much moister and cooler Iberia. The Portuguese laurel is accompanied by alder, narrow-leaved ash, strawberry tree and Portuguese heath. In the dense vegetation of the streams you can find a number of ferns, like soft shieldfern, Jersey fern, Irish spleenwort and broad bucklerfern. These ferns also occur in the warm, humid areas of northwestern Spain and southwestern Ireland.

The amphibian and reptile world changes with the increase in altitude. Midwife toads and grass snakes are central European species, which manage to survive here. Many other new species, however, are unique to the mountains of the Iberian Peninsula. In other words, they are very rare. This goes for the Almanzor fire salamander (a subspecies of the central European fire salamander), Schreiber's green lizard and parsley frog.

For those who are not that much into ferns, frogs or cloud forest relics, a walk along the mountain stream is certainly not a waste of time. The scenery is fabulous and the feel is very different from the safari-sensation of the lowlands.

Portuguese heath (top) and alders (bottom) form a ribbon of dense vegetation bordering the creeks in the mountains. The creek on the picture is the Almonte in the Villuercas Mountains (route 15).

Steppes

> The best routes in the steppes are the short trip near Trujillo (route 10) and espe-
> cially the long tour in La Serena (route 12). Other good routes are 8, 9 and 14.
> See page 191 for general tips on bird watching in the steppes.

Like a drab, brownish-yellow sea, the steppes of the Extremadura stretch
out in all directions from the town of Cáceres. In the hot summer, they
have a serene calm, with nothing more than grasshoppers chirping away
in the afternoon heat. Dead grass forms tufts around the *dientes de perros*
or dog's teeth -the typical, pointy rock sprigs that stick out of the poor soil
like bad dental work. The rock is of a very hard slate and the scantiest barrens have so many dog's teeth that the landscape is more like a deserted
graveyard than a grassland.
The extensive steppes cover around 10% over the total surface of the
Extremadura and have a charm very different from that of the dehesas:
desolate rather than pleasing, inhospitable rather than pretty.
Nevertheless, they make for beautiful scenery and host a fascinating
birdlife.

Steppes of la Serena

Genesis of the Steppes

However deserted and natural the grasslands of Extremadura may seem, they are just as much a man-made landscape as the dehesas are. In contrast to popular belief, they do not cover the driest regions of Extremadura, the ones that supposedly receive too little rain to support tree growth. On the contrary, most of the present-day grasslands of Extremadura were once covered by Mediterranean forests, just like the dehesas.

The steppes are not the result of land mismanagement either. A careless observer might conclude that recent erosion and intensification of land use has turned former pristine dehesa or forest into wasteland. This is not the case; land mismanagement is at most a minor contributor to the size of the steppes.

In contrast to dehesas, the steppe soil is completely defenceless against fierce deluges. This small valley is dry throughout the year. Only right after a winter cloudburst it turns into a wild river that washes away the thin soil.

The genesis of the grasslands is much more mundane than extreme drought or devastating desertification: most steppes originated in Roman times when the wood was needed to build the houses of the cities of Mérida, Trujillo and Cáceres. The area around these cities was deforested and turned into grain fields to feed the population. (Mérida and Badajóz are not surrounded by grasslands because they lie in the fertile floodplain of the Guadiana River).

In more recent history, several waves of deforestation created new steppes. Wars swept over the region, destroying formerly forested areas. The Spanish Armadas of the 16th century required wood as well, although this effect might be exaggerated: of the 132 warships of which the origin is known, only 22 were built with wood from Mediterranean Spain.

The pointy sprigs know as 'dog's teeth' are found in very poor soils and make some steppes virtually useless to farmers. In their shelter grow pink foxglove (page 91) and friar's cowl (inset).

How steppes work

The seasonal cycle of the steppes is pretty straightforward. In winter they are green and have, on overcast days, an almost Scottish appearance. Thousands of sheep nibble away on the juicy green. In March the steppes suddenly burst into flower. Seas of purple viper's bugloss, annual daisies, hawksbeard, purple sand-spurrey, tolpis, common stork's bill and other whidespread, short-living plants turn the grasslands into a giant bouquet. The infertile and often abandoned steppes are dotted with retama and Spanish white broom. The colourful period continues well into May. Then the flowers suddenly wither and leave nothing but yellow grass. The sheep are moved into the summer pastures, leaving the plains deserted. Throughout the summer the vegetation is dormant. Only golden thistle continues to flower, but with its spiny, scrawny appearance this plant only emphasises the summer's harshness. Only upon the arrival of the first autumn rains does the green reappear.

Just like the dehesa, the agricultural system of the steppes consists of three phases. The first phase is again the planting of grain -mostly wheat, oat and barley- and lucerne, the latter for the enrichment of the soil (lucerne produces nitrogen in its roots, which is good for other plants to grow). After the harvest, the land is left to lie fallow to recover. Lacking the shadow of the dehesa trees, the soil is more prone to desiccation. In order to diminish this process, the land is ploughed in for the warmer months. Ploughing destroys the small holes and pores in the soil through which the groundwater is able to evaporate. In the ploughed fields, seeds and grains come to the surface, much to the enjoyment of some birds. Calandra larks and corn buntings are drawn to the ploughed fields, as is a rarity like the black-bellied sandgrouse. The latter seems almost exclusive to this type of terrain.

In winter, the land turns to grassland and as such it is managed for a few years, depending on the fertility of the particular plot of land. Then the next cycle of ploughing and sowing starts.

Some parts of the steppes escape the cycle. Their poor soil and the presence of too many dog's teeth makes it not worth the effort of planting cereal. Some parcels have been abandoned altogether: the owner has died, moved away or retired from agriculture entirely. The second half of the 20th century witnessed a true exodus from Extremadura, allowing large tracts of land to turn into wasteland (see history section). These have slowly been filled in by spiny greenweed* and retama bushes, plants that seem to personify desolateness.

These bushy steppes often lose their value as bird sanctuaries, but become more interesting for small animals profiting from the increased cover, such as lizards and snakes.

Calandra larks (top) are found in all types of steppes, but prefer the more barren areas. Cereal plots (below) become the larger birds, such as Montagu's harrier and great bustard (page 115).

LANDSCAPE

The Spanish marbled white, here on a tolpis flower, is a common butterfly in the steppes and dehesas.

The flora and wildlife of the steppes

The flora of the steppes is similar to that of the open dehesas, but is generally less diverse. Some notable plants include the tiny pygmy evax*, globe-flowered steppe-edelweiss*, Iberian Jerusalem-sage* and hollow-stemmed asphodel. Between the dog's teeth, well-hidden from the grazing and trampling animals, you can find some more interesting plants. Especially numerous here are the pink foxglove*, and Friar's cowl, a relative of lords-and-ladies that flowers in winter and early spring (p.50).

The Extremaduran grasslands are renowned for their birdlife. Whereas remnant populations of rare grassland birds linger in the puszta reserves in Hungary and in the dry upland pastures in France, they flourish in the grasslands of Extremadura. Together with some other Spanish regions, Extremadura harbours the bulk of the European steppe birds. Large numbers of black-bellied and pin-tailed

The beautiful black-shouldered kite is a bird from Africa that invaded southwestern Spain in the 1950s.

sandgrouse, stone curlews and little bustards roam the treeless hills of La Serena and the plains between Cáceres and Trujillo, the prime grassland areas within Extremadura. To give an idea of the importance of the steppes as a bird sanctuary, in La Serena alone there are around 800 great bustards, 2,500 little bustards, just over 2,000 black-bellied sandgrouse and just under 2,000 of the pin-tailed variety.

Thekla and calandra larks occur in countless numbers, while corn buntings and stonechats are possibly even more numerous. Montagu's harriers fly low over the fields, scouting for mice, lizards, snakes, young birds and eggs.

The large eyes of the stone curlew unmask it as a night owl that keeps a low profile during the day.

Birds are not scattered over the steppes randomly. Rather, each species prefers a different type of steppe. In a way they are all connoisseurs, appreciating differences we can hardly recognise without considerable effort. The dog's teeth are used as perches by black-eared wheatears, little owls, hoopoes and southern grey shrikes. Insect-eating birds seeking out cover, such as little bustards, favour steppes with high grasses. Great bustards seek out the cereal plots, and so on.

In winter, the grasslands attract large numbers of birds fleeing the true northern cold in favour of the chilliness of the Extremaduran steppes. Tens of thousands of lapwings, golden plovers, meadow pipits and sky larks come down from northwestern Europe. Merlin and dotterel are visitors from central and northern Scandinavia, although they come in much smaller numbers.

Insects and sheep shape the ecosystem

Reptiles, insects and other large invertebrates occur in enormous numbers in the steppes. Most of them you won't find that easily. Scorpions, tarantulas and lizards live a hidden life underneath stones, bushes or in the ground. Only the grasshoppers are truly conspicuous, jumping all around you in the warmer months. They find safety in their numbers: there is no predator that can eat them all. The Moroccan locust in particular is known for its dramatic seasonal outbursts, turning patches of steppes into a giant, moving carpet of crickets.

Nymph of the hooded praying mantis*.

The presence of many small animals is a sign of a healthy ecosystem, since they form one of the most important food sources for birds. Great bustard chicks are reared on grasshoppers. For lesser kestrels and white storks, grasshoppers are the bulk food during summer. The collared pratincole grabs its prey on the wing. They eat pretty much any invertebrate that enters their airspace. Montagu's harriers catch lizards. Little owls, stone curlews, rollers, hoopoes, southern grey shrikes, bee-eaters... they all feed mainly on insects and lizards.

The importance of this group of animals for the steppe habitat became painfully clear in the 1980s when large-scale employment of the indiscriminatingly violent pesticide Malathion wiped out nearly the entire insect life. This was right before the harsh summer months. Probably millions of invertebrates died. Thousands of birds starved to death a little later. Fortunately, the use of Malathion is subject to strict regulations today.

Insects and lizards don't appear out of thin air either. They depend on micro-scale differences in the landscape, such as rocks, cracks and vegetation that continuously changes from herbs to grasses to shrubs and to open soil. Here they find both food and shelter.

In other places in Europe, such as on the aforementioned Hungarian Plain, many steppes have been converted into more intensively managed grasslands. The small-scale landscape differences and subsequently most of their bird, flora and insect life got thereby lost. In Extremadura the poor soils and massive size prevented this change. The steppes are still managed non-intensively and retain their value as a safe haven for the flora and fauna of the dry grasslands.

Other very important landscape shapers are the flocks of sheep traversing the steppes. In places where they come often, such as near the barns, grasses are nibbled away and inedible herbs prevail. These often have a high seed production, attracting seed-eating birds like larks and sandgrouse. In places where sheep come less frequently, grasses prevail, attracting insect-eating birds and bustards.

Sheep do not only shape the vegetation by eating away the grass. Through their dung they also sow the pastures anew, just like they do in the dehesas. And of course they die. With this final contribution, the steppes become decorated with one of its most scenic aspects: that lonely silhouette of a vulture against the big, deep-blue sky.

Sheep are the engine behind the steppe ecosystem.

Mediterranean evergreen forest

One of the best-preserved relicts of the Mediterranean evergreen forest in the western Mediterranean region can be found on the northern slopes of the Sierra the Corchuelas in Monfragüe. The most beautiful stretch is along route 3, but route 2 is best for observing the contrast between forest and dehesa vegetation. Route 4 offers some younger stands of evergreen forest.

The true untouched Mediterranean evergreen forest of the lowlands is rare and confined to remote areas of Monfragüe (routes 2 and 3).
Monfragüe's evergreen forests are unique not only within Extremadura, but within Europe as a whole. Beyond the borders of Extremadura, such forests are rare and mostly confined to the occasional small, isolated pocket in mountainous regions. The stretch in Monfragüe is thus of supreme value.
The Mediterranean forest is lush, scenic, pleasant and of interest to the visitor for a number of reasons. For one thing, the Mediterranean forest forms what is supposedly the primeval vegetation of the Mediterranean basin. Obviously, the forest found in Monfragüe cannot serve as a model for the entire Mediterranean region, but its structure -a dense, species-rich forest- is thought to have been predominant in the region before humankind altered the landscape (see text box on page 60).
The Mediterranean evergreen forest is very dense. Compared to central European forests with trees that reach up to forty metres, the Mediterranean forests are much lower, with trees not growing more than fifteen to twenty metres in height. Yet the diversity of trees and shrubs exceeds that of central European forests and the undergrowth has a good number of wildflowers.

North and south facing slopes

An eye-catching feature of the Mediterranean evergreen forests is the profound difference between the forest on north and south-facing slopes, a difference that is splendidly illustrated along route 2. On the northern slopes the canopy is dominated by cork oak and Lusitanian oaks, with strawberry tree, tree heath, laurustinus, Montpellier maple and turpentine tree playing second fiddle. There is not much of a herb layer under the shady canopy, yet the scattered plants together add up to a considerable number of plant species. Most conspicuous are Mediterranean selaginella and green-flowered birthwort*, which creep over the damp for-

est floor. Grassy patches are graced by the bright-yellow palmate anemone and spotted rockrose. Pallid narcissus* form delicate droplets along the trail and a number of orchids can be found if you pay close attention (see orchid section on page 97).

The north slopes (*umbría* in Spanish) are damp and cool. Rocks and tree stems are buried under thick blankets of moss, lichen and selaginella. An oddity for west- Europeans used to low heathlands is the tree heath, which reaches up to six metres. The stems of the tree heath look as if charred by fire, but closer inspection reveals that they are in fact covered entirely by a black fungus, which in turn is a good substrate to grow on for lichens. Underneath the soft green canopy of the heath, thousands of black, velvety stems and greyish-green lichens surround you. The fungus is not really a disease or an irregularly occurring event; all heaths become fungus-and-lichen covered and the plants seem to be unaffected by these uninvited subtenants.

Dense Mediterranean evergreen forest dominate the shady north slopes (umbría) of Monfragüe. Two typical species of this species-rich forest are laurustinus and three heath (top). Very remarkable are the black, fungus and lichen-covered stems of the tree heath (inset).

The south-facing slopes (*solana* in Spanish) receive much more direct sunlight and are consequently less damp. The vegetation is more open and to some extent resembles the dehesa. Holm oak is the dominant tree. In the space between, there is some pasture and many shrubs, including wild olive, lentisc, gum cistus, and retama. Red deer graze and wild boars rummage the topsoil, preventing the grassy patches from overgrowing. The wildflowers here are pink catchfly*, spotted rockrose, palmate anemone, southern daisy, tassel hyacinth and common asphodel (white asphodel frequents the north slope). Occasionally, you stumble upon some other, beautiful species, such as snakeshead and wild tulip (routes 1 and 3). You can find many of these species in the dehesa as well.

In general one could say that the evergreen Mediterranean forests form a refuge for those plants that can withstand more shade, but are not adapted to the chewing jaws of the goats and sheep.

Zonation in the evergreen forest

As is often the case with well-developed habitats, the landscape is only unified at first glance. A closer look reveals many different types of evergreen Mediterranean forest within 'the' evergreen Mediterranean forest. Exposure to the sun, presence of groundwater, and the depth of solid rock

Pallid narcissus, sometimes also referred to as angel's tears.

greatly determine the type of vegetation. In Monfragüe, areas covered with big rocks form open patches in the dense forest.

A general pattern in the forest can be distinguished as you descend from the ridge of the mountain to the bottom. The following small text will rush you downhill on paper, but we very much recommend doing it yourself in the field (route 2, and to a lesser extent route 3).

The highest region is reserved for a dense tangle of small holm oaks that grow out from between the rock cracks. Here, the soil is so thin that nothing else can grow. Further down, holm oak makes way for cork and Lusitanian oaks, which enjoy the deeper soils. They are dotted over the hills; the space between them is filled by a dense tangle of shrubs and small trees such as strawberry tree, tree heath and laurustinus. In certain spots, the heath forms thick tangles that close directly above your head, revealing the enchanting world of black stems (fungus) and soft-green lichens. In other places slate comes to the surface and trees cannot root. Here the forest opens up with French lavender, some brooms and spiny green-weed*.

The birdlife of the forest is remarkably central European. Most dehesa birds have made way for great and blue tits, robins, blackcaps and chaffinches (see text box on following page).

The vegetation changes again at the base of the mountain, where more or less permanent streams feed the soil. Dense tangles of winding plants like bramble, smilax, black bryony and wild vine border the stream in some spots, while other patches are kept open by deer and wild boar, which come down to drink and graze. These areas are grassy, with interesting wildflowers such as rosy garlic, tongue orchid and summer lady's-tresses.

Snakeshead, a rather rare plant of grassy, somewhat damp patches in scrubland and evergreen forest.

Birds and the puzzle of the original vegetation

The Mediterranean evergreen forest is believed to be the pristine vegetation of the Mediterranean basin, but its birdlife is very similar to that of the forests in central and northwestern Europe. Upon first thought this is surprising. In keeping with evolution theory, a sizable area with its own unique landscape features -like the Mediterranean evergreen forest- is expected to develop its own unique set of species over time. If it is indeed the original Mediterranean vegetation, there should have been enough time for a unique birdlife to evolve.

But the birds tell us otherwise. The bulk of the species occurring in the dense foliage are the robin, wren, blackbird, blackcap, chaffinch and blue, great and long-tailed tits; all of them are birds you probably also see around the bird feeder in your central-European garden.

In the absence of birds typical for the evergreen forest, one may wonder whether it dominated indeed the primeval landscape of southern Europe. Therefore, an increasing number of scientists challenge the idea of the forest-covered Mediterranean.

Moreover, there is not only disagreement on the primeval vegetation of the region, even the character of the landscape of more recent times is highly debated. Some sources claim that "even as recently as the sixteenth century the armies of Charles Quint travelled across Spain and France without ever leaving the shadow of the tree canopy"[1]. Meanwhile, others go to great lengths to show that the exact opposite is true and come to the conclusion that "the impression is of a distinctly more arid Spain [in Roman times] than today, at least in the south and east, the best known parts"[2]. Books are filled with studies trying to distil an image of the landscape from Roman and medieval documents. This is a difficult task, because the opinion of the writers of the old documents about what represents a forest may vary strongly. Even today you could say that Extremadura is forested-covered for over 50%, if you would call a dehesa a forest. If you don't, it would probably be no more than 5%. A historical account of the vegetation cover is even harder.

The question of what constituted the original and historical landscape is not only interesting in itself. It also says a lot about the human behaviour towards the environment. A widely accepted idea is that humankind has ruined the Mediterranean landscape, changing a lush and well-forested version of the gar-

[1] Blondel J., Aronson J., 1999. *Biology and wildlife of the Mediterranean region.* Oxford University Press.

[2] Grove A.T., Rackham O., 2003. *The Nature of Mediterranean Europe. An ecological history.* Yale University Press

den of Eden into a bone-dry withering bedrock with a few thorny bushes. However, if the original landscape was more like a scrubland or a savannah instead of a forest, then humankind was not as disastrous after all.

The birds seem to testify to the latter view. If the original landscape was a forest, wouldn't it be strange that the landscape with the thorny bushes has more unique bird species than the patches of lush Mediterranean evergreen forest. For example, on the crest of Monfragüe's Sierra de las Corchuelas (where the castle stands; route 2) you can find rock bunting, blue rock thrush, black and black-eared wheatears, all of them Mediterranean specialties. It would take these species quite a lot more than a few hundred years to evolve and adapt to this environment. So it cannot be that these landscapes were not part of the original landscape.

So an explanation for the presence of central-European birds in the evergreen forests could be that these forests are not the original vegetation at all. But an alternative answer is found in the history of the ice ages. In these times the temperate forest was pushed southwards into the Mediterranean basin. When the warmth came back these forests retreated to the new temperate zones in central Europe and with them moved the birds belonging there. However, in part they lingered on in suitable spots in the Mediterranean region, such as the evergreen forest. Evolution theory dictates that for a species to evolve from another species, it has to be separated from the original species (like the two azure-winged magpies, see text box on page 107). This never happened with the forest birds, and therefore you can find our garden birds in the Mediterranean forest.

In contrast, the typical Mediterranean birds evolved in many different spots. Most of them are scrubland birds. According to the people who claim that the evergreen forest covered the Mediterranean plains, scrubland was limited to the mountains. The Mediterranean is full of isolated mountain ranges and Extremadura is no exception. Every isolated mountain range could evolve its own scrubland bird. When the scrublands later invaded the lowlands, due to human activity, these birds descended and mixed to form a diverse community. So in the end, the present-day birdlife of the Mediterranean still can be explained either way. One thing is clear, though. Scrublands, Mediterranean evergreen forests and savannahs like the dehesas contribute today to the ecological richness of the Extremadura, regardless of whether they were part of the original vegetation or not.

The Mediterranean forest as a refuge

The evergreen forest is not only interesting in its own right, but it also has a firm ecological connection to the surrounding dehesas and steppes. It is much like the way suburbia is connected to the nearest business park. Animals that hunt in the dehesas and steppes find a refuge in the forest. This goes for deer and wild boar as well, but even more so for birds of prey. For example, the roughly six-by-thirty kilometre stretch constituting Monfragüe's Nature Park holds over 250 pairs of black vultures. They all live off the carcasses of cattle and game. The vultures can soar up and wander as far as to 200 kilometres away from their nests. They are commonly found scavenging in the steppes around Trujillo and Cáceres. A similar story goes for the eleven pairs of Spanish imperial eagles and the numerous short-toed eagles. All of them breed in the giant, old cork oaks deep in the forest. (The other vultures and eagles breed on rocks, but they too wander off into the surrounding lowlands.)

The Mediterranean forest also forms a refuge for the Iberian lynx. This large cat is one of the rarest and most secretive of all mammals and only occurs in the southwestern part of the Iberian Peninsula. No one has the slightest idea about the population density of the lynx, only that it probably occurs in the most remote parts of the Mediterranean evergreen forests.

The mountains

Mountains of up to 1,600 metres are found in the Sierra de Las Villuercas (routes 15 and 16), La Vera and Valle de Jerte (routes 17 and 18) and the area known as Sierra de Gata / Las Hurdes, which is not included in this guidebook. The only route with high mountain characteristics is route 18. Lower mountain ranges with often dramatic, rocky cliffs and escarpments can be found in Monfragüe (routes 1, 2, and 4), and La Serena (route 13).

The Sierra de Gata, La Vera, Valle de Jerte and Sierra de las Villuercas are high enough to support a profoundly different climate compared to the lowlands. As a result, you will find yourself in a completely different world up there. In spring, summer and autumn, the temperatures are more agreeable, there is more rainfall, creeks don't dry out and the vegetation is green well into the summer. Winters are short but cool, and at higher altitudes it snows during the coldest months.

Unlike the rock-dwelling griffon vulture, the black vulture builds massive nests on trees. They are largely dependent on old cork oaks, which are present in the Mediterranean evergreen forests and at the base of the mountains.

LANDSCAPE

The castle of Cabañas del Castillo, on top of a rugged mountain ridge in the Sierra de las Villuercas (route 15).

The vegetation responds accordingly. No longer is the summer the obvious violent season to plants -winter is known to show its teeth. Evergreen oaks no longer have the upper hand and deciduous trees, such as Pyrenean oak, enter the scene. The dehesas make way for a new sort of orchard: the chestnut grove. Together with Pyrenean oak forests, scrubland and cherry groves, the chestnut groves comprise the lovely landscape of the Extremaduran mountains.

A patchwork of landscapes

The mountains show a patchwork of different landscapes. At the base of the mountain you find olive groves and dehesas dominated by cork oak and, to a lesser extent, Lusitanian oak. Their location at the foot of the mountains indicates a moister climate and deeper soil, offering better growing conditions than on the plains. As a consequence, dehesa trees are often larger. There are massive cork oaks and sweet chestnuts, some of which are over 500 years old. The wildlife in this dehesa is richer than in the holm oak version in the lowlands.

Two conspicuous plants of the forests and dehesas in the mountains: the Spanish bluebell and western peony (facing page).

Higher up the slopes you find Pyrenean oak forests and chestnut groves, alternating with dense scrubland. This is a lush and green landscape in spring and summer, with decorative lichens hanging from the branches. Because the trees shed their leaves each year, the forest soil is covered with a thick layer of humus, much like in central European forests but unlike the dehesa soil.

The rocky crests of the mountains are either barren or overgrown with prickly juniper and holm oak. The presence of holm oak here is a bit surprising, because one would expect evergreen trees to have a hard time at higher altitudes. The challenge the holm oaks face here is shown by their small, gnarled branches, which are heavily decorated with lichens. Yet they can survive here and have no competition from other trees because of the thin, dry soil. When mountains reach over 1,600 metres in height, it becomes too cold for the holm oak and scrubland takes over.

Western peony

Rocky outcrops

The rock escarpments are favoured nesting sites for birds. Overhanging rocks provide shelter against wind and rain, while the warm, rising winds stroking the south-facing cliffs are perfect for large-winged birds to take off. Many cliff-dwelling birds are large predators that profit from the warm rising air to take flight.

With this in mind, a mere glance at the map of Extremadura is enough to explain the region's unsurpassed numbers of rock-dwelling birds, such as griffon and Egyptian vultures, eagle owls and golden and Bonelli's eagles: the whole of Extremadura is laced through with low to medium-sized rocky mountain chains, which are surrounded by lowlands full of prey.

Griffon vultures are without doubt the most numerous and visible. They breed in colonies varying from a few nests to gatherings of over 50 pairs, such as the famous one at the Peñafalcon in Monfragüe (routes 1 and 2). The Bonelli's eagle is another typical cliff dweller. About 70% of the Spanish population of this rare eagle breeds in the Extremaduran mountains. It is very territorial and goes to great lengths in order to defend its nest. The story goes that a Bonelli's eagle once attacked and killed a black vulture, simply because it came too close to its nest.

Other rock dwellers are golden eagles, Egyptian vultures, eagle owls, pere-grine falcons, common kestrels, ravens, Alpine swifts, crag martins, red-rumped swallows, red-billed choughs and blue rock thrushes. The bird community of the rocks is largely independent of the altitude. Colonies of griffon vultures occur in small rocky ranges in the lowlands, but also 2,000 metres up in the Sierra de Gredos. This is not the case for the plant life, which changes in correspondence with the altitude. What remains the same at every altitude, however, is that the rocks host a good number of botanical rarities. To give an example, at low and mid-altitude ranges you can find the broom-like Spanish adenocarpus*, unique to southwestern Iberia. At higher altitudes, the rock cracks are the place to find the Gredos' snapdragon*, which only occurs in the Sierra de Gredos.

Red-rumped swallows build igloo-shaped nests that are pasted upside down on over-hanging cliffs. The nests are made of mud the swallow collects from rain puddles.

Pyrenean oak forests and chestnut groves

The larger part of the mountain slopes is covered by ancient, open chest-nut groves and young Pyrenean oak forests. Both have a closed canopy and give the visitor the feel of walking through a real forest. On warm days, when the plains are stifled by a paralysing heat, life is agreeable when taking it easy under the canopy of the Pyrenean oaks.

The Pyrenean oak forest forms the original vegetation of the mountain slopes. Unfortunately, from a naturalist's point-of-view most of today's forests are not much to write home about: young stands of dense, even-aged forest with a poor birdlife and a thick cover of bracken fern. There are few wildflowers, save the bright-blue shrubby gromwell (p.19), and a poor, rather mundane birdlife. For deer, wild boar and badger, however, the dense cover of this forest provides a very good retreat.

The older, more pristine Pyrenean oak forests can only be found on the high, mostly inaccessible slopes of La Vera. If you take into account that Spain is a country with very few timber trees, it is hardly surprising that in the past the Pyrenean oak forests were primarily used for wood production. This changed in the 1950s, when many people moved away from the mountains and those remaining switched from fire wood to butane gas. Many groves, scrublands and meadows turned into Pyrenean oak forest, which accounts for the large number of young trees.

In contrast to the Pyrenean oak forest, the chestnut groves are often centuries old. There is even one giant chestnut of approximately 800 years old (see picture on following page). This tree, like all Extremaduran chestnuts, is not very high. It is pruned from a very young age. Only the impressively massive trunk of almost three metres in diameter reveals the age of the tree.

For a nature enthusiast, the groves are very interesting, even though the chestnut itself is probably not even native to Spain. The natural distribution of the sweet chestnut is not entirely certain, but it probably did not reach far beyond Italy until the Romans came and dragged it all over their empire.

The chestnut groves on a sun-soaked spring morning. The soil is graced by swathes of Sicilian orchids.

The forest floor of the chestnut groves is light, open and rich in flowers. Plant enthusiasts will be delighted to see so many orchids. The pale yellow Sicilian orchid, narrow-leaved helleborine and early purple orchid are most numerous. They rarely fail to appear and sometimes even occur by the thousands. In early spring, Spanish bluebell, cowslip and Fernandes's narcissus* and pallid narcissus* form colourful dots in the groves. As spring proceeds, another botanical jewel, the western peony (p. 65), unfolds its delicate rose-like flowers. It is most common in the lower reaches of the mountains, growing under cork oak dehesas and on the edges of chestnut groves.

The oldest tree known in Extremadura is the Chestnut of Temblar, near the village of Segura de Toro. It is estimated to be 800 years old, is only 19 metres high, but has a trunk circumference of 9 metres.

The more excited the plant watcher gets, the more glum the birdwatcher becomes. Sometimes it seems as if birds and plants don't like each other. As soon as the interesting mountain flora starts to appear, the exotic birdlife of the Extremaduran plains is replaced by one more sober, or at least more central European. Chaffinches, great and blue tits, Bonelli's warblers, spotted flycatchers, nuthatches and short-toed treecreepers form the bulk of the birds in the chestnut groves and Pyrenean oak forests. Other typical species are the honey-buzzard and wryneck, both of which reach the southern edge of their distribution range in Extremadura.

Higher still: high-altitude scrubland

In between the Pyrenean oak forests and chestnut groves, there are also large areas with scrublands, mostly consisting of gum cistus, Spanish and umbel-flowered* heaths and common and Spanish white brooms.

But higher up in the mountains, roughly above 1,600 metres, the woods give way to another vegetation zone. Within Extremadura, this vegetation is only present in the highest region of the Sierra de Gredos. It is hard to climb up to this altitude from the Extremaduran side of the Gredos Mountains, and it is therefore not included in our routes. However, we will give a very short description of these alpine scrublands for those wishing to go around the Gredos Mountains and visit them from the north (see 'nearby destinations worth a visit' on page 192).

The highest regions of the Gredos mountains are dominated by rock barrens and piorno broom* scrubland. The broom flowers in late May and June and turns the entire upper region of the mountains yellow, a brilliant sight.

Birds of interest are the rock thrush and the wallcreeper. Hortolan bunting breeds on the margins of the numerous creeks. A true eyecatcher is the bluethroat. This typical breeding bird of central European reedbeds occupies the piorno broom* scrubland and is common in the Gredos mountains. The Iberian ibex and the Iberian rock lizard (p. 119) are the non-avian star species of the high mountains. Both are unique to the high mountains of Spain.

Iberian ibex and piorno broom* are typical of the high slopes of the Gredos Mountains.

History

Whether you regard the history of Extremadura from a geological or from a human perspective, it goes back a long way. Together with the *mesetas*, or central Spanish uplands, the bedrock of Extremadura belongs to the oldest in all of Europe. It is part of a broad belt formed during the Hercynian era, between 300 and 400 million years ago. The belt runs from western Iberia through France (Vosges), Belgium (Ardennes), Germany (Black Forest, Harz) and southwestern England and Ireland. The bedrock is very hard, but 300 million years is a long time, enough to take most edges off the rock and to create the rolling hills of Extremadura. It is also sufficient time for rivers to cut deep into the solid soil, never to change their courses again.

The passing of history at the Almonte River near Jaraicejo: the old medieval bridge, with in the background two newer ones, both built in the 20th century. The third bridge is the one of the Madrid - Mérida highway.

Creation of steppes and dehesas

Neolithic men settled on the plains and in the mountain chains of Extremadura some 7,000 years ago. They lived in small groups and hunted in the valleys, while staying in caves in the numerous mountain chains. In several spots, rock paintings from this period serve as silent reminders of Neolithic man (routes 2 and 13). Several dolmen have been found as well, they served as artificial caves in the plains further away from the mountains.

The neolithic age also marks the period when humankind started to add agriculture to its ways of living. In the course of time this led to a thinning of the original Mediterranean forest and to the creation of the savannah-like dehesa landscape. Indeed, the first evidence of a dehesa-like agricultural system stems from approximately 4,000 years ago. This probably

also had a positive effect on the numbers of game. Deer and wild boar thrive in areas where there is not only dense foliage for cover, but also open pasture for grazing.

Extremadura saw big changes with the coming of the Romans, who conquered the region in 206 BC. Some remarkably intact remains of Roman structures can still be found in Mérida, which was just as much a capital then as it is now. In fact, it was the capital of all of Lusitania, a Roman province which encompassed Extremadura and a very large part of present-day Portugal. In Mérida (Augusta Emerita in Roman times) you will find one of the most intact Roman amphitheatres in the world and the largest Roman bridge in all of Spain (with breeding alpine and pallid swifts and crag martins; just next to the bridge is a mixed colony of cattle egrets and night herons).

Apart from Mérida, other Roman cities were built, such as Cáceres and Trujillo. For the construction of these towns the builders needed wood -a lot of it. The dehesa and woodland surrounding the settlements were cut down, the timber was used for construction and the land was converted to crop and grain fields. This heralded the birth of the steppes of Extremadura. With the founding of these cities, the creation of the steppes and the previous emergence of the dehesas, the blueprint for Extremadura's present-day landscape was largely finished. The typical division between urban life and the largely uninhabited surrounding plains (the magical-sounding *despoblados*) also crystallized during this time.

Another famous construction in the region is the Ruta de la Plata, a Roman road cutting straight through the entire western part of Spain, from Asturias in the north to Seville in the south. Ruta de la Plata literally means 'silver route', but this is a corruption of an Arab word, 'ballata', which is not a reference to silver at all, but to the cobbled pavement. The fact that it was paved over such an incredible length, over vast, empty uplands and through steep mountains, made it a vital contribution to trade within western Spain and, through the port of Seville, with the rest of the world. Extremadura was at that time an area of significance.

The Visigoths and the Moors

After the withdrawal of the Romans, Spain was invaded by several Germanic tribes. To regain control, the Roman emperor commissioned the Visigothic king, who was married to his daughter, to restore order. In return the Visigoths received the right to settle there and govern the country. The highly romanised Visigoths were a warrior elite, which left the civil administration to the Romans; Latin remained the language of government and commerce. The Visigoths have left little traces in Extremadura, contrary to their successors, the Moors. After their landing at Gibraltar in 711, it took them only a few years to conquer Spain, with the exception of the northwest, which they were not able to subdue.

During the Moorish rule Extremadura went through a second prosperous period, culturally as well as agriculturally. The Moors introduced citrus fruits, melons and state-of-the-art irrigation. They also created some military constructions, such as the fort of Al-Monfrag, the present-day Castillo de Monfragüe (route 2). In spite of Extremadura's progress, the region lost its important position in relation to other parts of Spain, in particular to Andalusia.

The Christian lords have built many castles on rocky hilltops in Extremadura. This is the castle of Belvis de Monroy, with the Gredos Mountains in the background.

The power of the Mesta

Moorish rule ended after seven centuries in a series of gruesome wars, collectively known as the Reconquista. Monfragüe was one of the battlefields, because it controlled one of the very few crossings over the River Tagus.

Statue of Francisco
Pizarro on the Plaza
Mayor in Trujillo.

The Spanish crown divided Extremadura amongst a small group of royals and Christian leaders. This was probably the beginning of the large landownership that has been typical of the region up to this day. With this new division, the poverty and dependency among the local residents increased. They became serfs to their masters, the *Señoritos*. Although officially the feudal system was abolished in the 19th century, the dependency on land owners continued well into the 20th. If you can get your hands on it, the award-winning movie '*los Santos Inocentes*' provides fascinating insight in the incredible dependency of the Extremaduran land workers on the rich landowners in the middle of the 20th century. It is also a beautiful and unexpected portrait of the bleak Extremaduran winter landscape.

Since the middle ages, the huge estates have been used to raise merino sheep for their wool and meat. The wool became one of Spain's prime export products. The large sheep breeders and keepers united themselves to form the *Mesta*, an organisation with near-supreme power. It was during the heyday of the *Mesta* that large-scale transhumance became operational (see text box on page 76). The *Mesta* created the system of drover roads, known as *cañadas*. Drover roads are better described as drover strips, since a *cañada* had (and officially still has) a law-enforced width of 75 metres.

The days of the *Mesta* also marked the birth of the word *'dehesa'*. Dehesa comes from *'defensa'*, or 'fenced terrain' and originally had nothing to do with a landscape type. It refers to the privately owned parcels, the fenced-off terrain, bordering the *cañada*. Before the word 'dehesa' came into play, the wood pastures were usually called *encinar* (holm oakery), or *monte hueco* (gapped forest).

An old stonewall forms the fence of the old *cañada* north of Trujillo. Note the difference in grazing pressure between the public land left of the wall and the privately owned land on the right side. In the days of the *Mesta* the situation was likely reversed, with high grazing pressure on the *cañada* and low grazing pressure on the private land.

While the *Mesta* and its members thrived, the living conditions of most Extremaduran people were poor. This poverty is often seen as the reason for so many Extremadurans to join the conquests of the Americas in the 15th and 16th century. Indeed, many of the famous conquistadores came from Extremadura. Francisco Pizarro was the most successful. The story goes that he grew up as a poor boy tending swine near Trujillo, but grew to be the leader of the fleet that conquered Peru and wiped out the Inca Empire in the process. Francisco de Orellana also came from Trujillo and

La Matanza

It is a brisk morning in November. The sun isn't yet fully up and you are lying in your comfortable bed in your *casa rural*. Your peaceful dreams of flocks of cranes flying through the crispy autumn air are unpleasantly disrupted by a bone-shattering squeal. You rush out onto your little balcony overlooking a village street and look right into the eyes of a dying pig, lying on a wooden table with blood gushing from a deep cut in its throat.

This is the other side of the picturesque country life.

La matanza means 'the slaughter' and is the period in which the villagers slaughter their pigs and make their hams, sausages and *manteca*. The latter is a mixture of pig fat and intestines mixed together and spiced up to make a fine breakfast sandwich spread (if your stomach can take it) popular in the southern part of Extremadura.

The *matanza* takes place between November and January, when the pigs have been fattened by the acorns and the temperatures are low enough to prevent the meat from getting spoiled.

explored much of the Amazon and Ecuador. Hernán Cortez, from the small Extremaduran village of Medellin, went to Central America and overthrew the empire of the Aztecs.

While grand civilizations in South and Central America tasted defeat at the hands of Spanish explorers, Trujillo and Cáceres grew in these days. The Extremaduran captains brought back treasures, and some massive houses were built with the riches of the Incas.

But this is the history of the large cities, of international politics and wealthy families -history as it went on between town walls. Outside, in the wide *despoblados* of steppes and dehesas, the centuries passed with the bleating of sheep, the call of the hoopoe, the pruning of the oaks and undoubtedly with generations of little swine-tending boys dreaming of becoming Francisco Pizarro. The dehesas quietly went through their cycles of winter grazing and summer slumber and through their cycles of sowing grain one year, followed by a fallow year and a couple of years of grazing, before cutting back the scrub and planting grain again (see page 31 for a description of the dehesa cycle). Notwithstanding some drastic social and economic changes during the 18th and 19th century, the general functioning of the dehesa remained undisturbed.

Transhumance: forgotten practise, forgotten culture

For centuries the shepherds in Spain have been on the move, following the seasons in search of green pasture for their sheep. They moved from the lowlands in winter to the high mountains in summer: long journeys through wild country full of wolves and thieves. These journeys are called 'transhumance', a phenomenon that is largely unknown to the public at large, but which had a profound impact on the lives and culture of the Spanish countryside and on the Mediterranean region as a whole.

Transhumance is the logical pastoral answer to the Mediterranean climate. The climate in the lowlands encourages plant growth only in winter and spring, but geology offers numerous high mountains where the situation is reversed and meadows are juicy during the summer months. Shepherds responded to this by adopting a migrant lifestyle, moving back and forth from the lowland winter pastures to the upland summer pastures: transhumance (see picture on page 79).

The word 'transhumance' is derived from the Latin words *trans* (through, over) and *humus* (land). It was first used in Spanish, where *'transhumar'* is employed as a verb. In Spain, sheep husbandry and thus transhumance was an especially important phenomenon because of the power of the sheep-owners guild, or *Mesta*. For a long time, tending sheep was important not only for poor peasants. Sheep meant money and power. The wool of the merino sheep, typical of Spain and southern France, was one of the most valuable products in Europe and brought great wealth to the bigwigs of the *Mesta* and to the Spanish Crown.

The transhumance moves over special drover roads, called *cañadas*. They are not like your average trail. *Cañadas* are very long, extending from the Extremaduran and Andalusian plains to the Cantabrian mountains in northwestern Spain. At set points along the drove roads are stops, *paradores*: simple hostels that provide a basic meal and shelter to the herdsman. The *parador* (Spanish for 'stopping place') was a phenomenon throughout Spain. Nowadays, the name has gratefully been borrowed by the state for their hotel chain. This present-day *parador* is a luxurious hotel not at all reminiscent of the traditional one.

There are ten royal *cañadas* in Spain, and all of them measure 75 metres in width to provide both space and food for the passing sheep. This size has been set by law. To get to the *cañada*, shepherds used smaller drover roads, known as *cordeles* (37.5 metres wide) and *veredas*. If you add them all up, the figures become quite impressive. The total length of drover roads in Spain amounts to 124,000 kilometres, with a surface of about 500,000 hectares of land.

The transhumance trip from Extremadura was long and harsh, going from the lowlands of Extremadura through the Gredos Mountains and the endless highlands of Castilla León, finally ending at the green mountains of Asturias and Cantabria. Along the way the herdsman had to deal with heat, snakebites and sheep straying from the herd. At night, the wolves came in hope of an easy prey. To withstand these dangers a number of customs and safety measures were adopted. Mastin dogs, big fellows, were bred especially to guard the herd from wolves. They were armoured with thick, spiked iron collars to defend themselves against wolf bites. The drover dogs were of the small, barking variety.

Today transhumance has become an endangered custom. The first big blow to the tradition came from an unexpected corner: Australia. This massive continent was perfect for breeding sheep. The wool of Australia flooded the market and the value of Merino wool plummeted, marking the end of the sheep-tending heyday.

Still, transhumance remained an important part of Extremaduran life until well into the second half of the 20th century. The remaining flocks of sheep still moved away in summer and the cleansing autumn rains were still intrinsically linked with the first clanging bells of returning sheep.

What did the traditional transhumance in for good were the sudden increase in wages and the increasing difficulties with landowners. When transhumance became a thing of the past, the broad *cañadas* were gradually incorporated into private land or disappeared beneath the asphalt. For in a country where most of the land is privately owned, building roads is easiest on the existing strips of public land. The road between Trujillo and Torrejón el Rubio, for example, follows the *cañada* for a while. You can still see this south of Torrejón, where the walls and fences separating the private lands are much further away from the road.

So is transhumance now dead and buried? It is hard to tell. The dehesas still do not provide sufficient pasture for the sheep and probably never will. But under current economic conditions it will always be cheaper to buy food than to move livestock. The original law allowing free passage for cattle over the *cañadas* is still maintained. The Spanish nature organisation 'Fondo Patrimonio Natural Europeo' demonstrated this vividly in 1995 when the flock of 2,000 sheep belonging to the organisation walked a *cañada* that leads straight through the centre of Madrid. Most shepherds who still practise transhumance today, do it differently. They take a truck and drive the cattle up into the mountains. This is transhumance modern style: no more bells accompanying the autumn rains, but the humming of truck engines.

The Crisis of the Dehesa

Major problems started in the 1950s and 60s. International markets for dehesa products like wool and meat either collapsed or found other sources. The price of merino sheep wool, once the cornerstone of Spanish agriculture and the cork on which the whole *Mesta* had floated, plummeted because of cheap, high-quality wool from Australia. The demand for wool in general also diminished, due to the rise of other types of fabric. Meanwhile, the prices of meat and other dehesa products decreased and the wages of land workers increased sharply.

This resulted in an exodus of Extremaduran people to other parts of Spain and abroad to France, Germany and the Netherlands, searching for work or a better income. Some regions, such as the area of Torrejón, lost over 50% of its inhabitants. Some dehesas and steppes were left without management and turned into wasteland. Other dehesas survived through the increase of meat production, causing overgrazing and neglect of the tree layer.

Meanwhile, Franco had some tricks up his sleeve to solve Extremadura's problems. His strategy of 'colonisation of the inlands' involved making some rigorous changes to the ailing Extremaduran agriculture. The entire fertile plain of Badajóz and Mérida was irrigated and changed into crop fields. Massive new reservoirs arose to quench the thirst of the new agriculture. The steep river valleys used for this purpose were also perfect for the construction of hydro-electrical works. In the narrow valley, water levels could be raised so as to create enormous pressure and thus a lot of electricity. Thousands of hectares of dehesa and whole dwellings disappeared under water. (The newly built chapel of Talaván (route 6) is a witness to this. The old one on the northern bank of the river has disappeared under water).

Paper was to be another of the pillars of Extremadura's economy. To this end, dehesas and remnant patches of forest were to make way for Eucalyptus plantations, the raw material for paper pulp. The rivers were to carry away the poisoned waters resulting from the paper-bleaching process.

Fortunately, most of the Eucalyptus plantations never became reality. Massive protests in the Monfragüe area that had also been marked to be planted with Eucalyptus resulted in the abandonment of the plan, paving the way for conservation of the area. The protests were international and people from all over Europe contributed to the purchase of the land of the present-day Monfragüe nature park, thus ensuring its conservation.

Nature conservation

Extremadura is a splendid region because of its scenery and ecology, because of its famous birdlife and equally rich flora and because of its wildlife and rare species of reptiles and amphibians. But that is not all. Just diving into the fascinating nature conservation issues of this region makes a trip to Extremadura worthwhile. Granted, this would be more of a scholarly trip, not as much fun as hiking or birdwatching, but intriguing and eye-opening nonetheless.

One of the last trans-huming herds travel-ling the *cañada* through Monfragüe.

What makes it so interesting is that Extremaduran nature conservation is very different from that of the great national parks in Europe or other continents. In Extremadura threats to nature encompass much more than nature alone. Its natural value is tightly linked to traditional agricultural practices. Today, the long-lasting marriage between extensive agriculture and nature is showing cracks. Its fine offspring of rich rural traditions and healthy populations of numerous rare plants and animals could be dragged down into the slipstream of this crisis.
In a nutshell, Extremadura faces the following problems:

Disruption of the dehesa system
The centuries-old agricultural system of the dehesas (see page 32) slowly started to come apart during the rule of Franco, from the 1950s onwards. Yet blaming it all on a dictator who has already been deemed a black page

in Spanish history would be a little too easy. Most troubles were and still are caused by changes in international markets and by an over-zealous ideology of rural development advocated by governments of all levels. A thorn in the side of nature conservation is the EU system of subsidising agriculture practises, which focus entirely on increasing production. Farmers are paid per head of livestock: the more sheep you have, the more money you receive, regardless of the state the animals are in. The over-grazing of the dehesas is the obvious result (these per-head subsidies have been abolished very recently).

Overgrazing is one of the main environmental problems of the dehesa.

It is hard to think of a system more at odds with the idea of maintaining a healthy balance between nature and agriculture than this one. In summer, high-protein fodder is brought in from elsewhere to feed the animals, because this is cheaper and easier than going through the cycle of

transhumance (text box on page 76). Animals remain on the dehesas year-round, nibbling away anything edible. The whole agriculture-pasture-forestry system, with its cycle of grain, pasture and scrub periods (see page 32 and text box on page 30), is going by the wayside.
Overgrazing obviously causes the disappearance of edible herbs and grasses, but it also stops the rejuvenation of the oaks of the dehesa. Young oaks amongst the older ones are becoming rare. The older oaks are less often pruned. Pruning is too time-consuming, and thereby too costly, in comparison to the products -branches for charcoal and leaves for fodder- it yields.

Water consumption and climate change
Spain is thirsty. The already unpredictable rainy season of the Mediterranean region has become even more unpredictable. Setting aside differences in opinion on how much of this is actually caused by current human-induced climate change, the tendency towards higher temperatures and more erratic deluges is obvious. Yet water consumption has increased sharply in Spain. Higher living standards and a tidal wave of summer tourists increase the demand for water. More hidden but even more wasteful in terms of water consumption is modern agriculture.
These problems are present all over Spain and some of them apply more to Andalusia, Catalonia and the arid southeast than to Extremadura. But the search for water is a national problem and will certainly be treated as such, which means that Extremadura's last free-flowing streams are greatly threatened.
Very recently, the beautiful Almonte River has been targeted for damming, in this case to take care of the dwindling water supply of booming Cáceres. As far as we know the proposed dam has been rejected for the moment, but the plan still exists, waiting for thirstier days.

Road building
New roads bring people into formerly quiet areas, create roadkill and form barriers for large animals. The recent road-building frenzy, partly financed by EU subsidies, has taken on insane proportions. It partly consisted in the renewal of already existing roads, but others cut through formerly pristine areas.
The intensification of traffic and road-building in previously intact terrain puts pressure on animals that depend on large, undisturbed areas, such as the great bustard, the Iberian lynx and the Spanish imperial eagle. More noticeably, the new roads have a negative aesthetic impact -and why should this not be a valid problem? The thick broad strips of asphalt, with

the complex systems of slip roads and roundabouts, don't seem to belong in quiet, rural Extremadura, with its centuries-old stone walls and majestic holm oaks (which are often ruthlessly cleared to broaden the road). Set aside aesthetic issues, the new roads are a menace to nature tourists. The edges of the asphalt almost tower above the shoulder of the road, making it impossible to pull over on the roadside. Stopping on the road proper to look at a hoopoe or a bee-eater is not an option either, because the smooth asphalt tempts your fellow road-users to speeding.

Newly built road road to Serrejón, cutting through formerly undisturbed dehesa. This picture was taken in 1996; the road is now a section of route 1.

The challenge for nature conservation

Extremadura is one of southern Europe's prime examples of semi-nature: an ancient landscape moulded by both man and nature in a finely balanced interplay. The dehesa was never meant to be the ecological refuge it has become. It was and still is the most logical way of conducting agriculture in the region, given the climate and the quality of the soil.

Whether you traverse the endless dehesas, the rolling steppeland or the rugged mountains, you can always find traces of human use, but rarely of human abuse (and the ones you do find are from the last 50 years). In a continent such as Europe, with a human history dating back to the dawn of time, this is a type of landscape and land use that should be cherished. In a time in which sustainability has (or should) become a major social goal, examples of areas that still maintain a sustainable lifestyle should be fostered.

Extremadura still offers a glance into the workshop of sustainability. You will not only see the unquestionably masterful result of sustainable land use, but also its practical problems, the threats and all the unromantic and even harsh aspects.

To protect nature in Extremadura by fencing it off, like in your average national park, won't work. The dehesas are already fenced off -in fact this is just what the word 'dehesa' originally meant. In Extremadura efforts should be directed at maintaining the traditional land use that is threatened by the free market.

Nature conservation organisations and regional and European governments are taking these threats seriously. Whereas the European and Extremaduran governments pose the problems themselves in the form of building roads and intensifying agriculture practises, they also work in counteracting the adverse effects. Dehesas are now part of the European Natura 2000 network of protected habitats, and hundreds of thousands of hectares of farmland in Extremadura are now managed in accordance with organic agriculture principles. The per-head subsidies for cattle were abolished in 2003, counteracting some of the overgrazing problems. What's more, sustainable food production is encouraged and nature education is an important element in the school program. Just about all schoolchildren are marched off into the mountains to get acquainted with their natural heritage. Ecotourism is also strongly promoted as an alternative means of income.

This also implies that you could help out a little by buying local dehesa products. Stretching the truth somewhat, you could say that you are protecting nature by eating Iberian ham. In this way ecotourism as a whole is a means of bringing money into the region without having to lose the dehesas. They have become valuable again.

FLORA AND FAUNA

Flora and fauna

While hikers, travellers and peace-seekers are just beginning to find their way to Extremadura, birdwatchers, nature photographers and ecologists discovered the region decades ago. To them, Extremadura ranks among the top regions in Europe. And with good reason, for the dehesas, steppes, rivers and mountains of Extremadura host a superb flora and fauna that is in several ways unique in the world.

The flora and fauna of the region are characterised by their so-called 'Lusitanian-Mediterranean' character: most the plants and animals have a typical Mediterranean distribution, but several are confined to a very small region of southwestern Iberia known as the Lusitanian region. You won't find them anywhere else in the entire world. A glance at the species list in the back of this book reveals the surname *'lusitanica'* quite often in the column of scientific names.

The Lusitanian region is quite isolated. Further east of the region lie the Spanish uplands with a much harsher climate, to the south and southeast the climate becomes more arid and to the far north it becomes temperate. The geology of Spain isolates the southwest from the rest of the country, giving it a unique climate with a unique flora and fauna.

Many Lusitanian species are plants, such as spiny greenweed* and Spanish adenocarpus*. But more well-known birds and animals also belong to this group, some of which are high on the must-see list of most travellers. Take the azure-winged magpie for example (text box on page 107). And of course there are two of the rarest and most beautiful animals in the world: the Spanish imperial eagle and the Iberian lynx.

The key to this division lies partly in the climate, but mainly in the geography of Spain. Although the climate is primarily Mediterranean, it has some strong Atlantic influences. Moist air drifts inland from the Ocean

The red-legged partridge is common in the scrublands, dehesas and steppes of Extremadura.

and empties out over mountains such as the Sierra de Gata, the Sierra de Gredos and the Sierra de las Villuercas. The latter mountain range hosts a handful of particularly interesting relicts from the Tertiary period, a bygone age in which moist cloud forests dominated the region. The most famous relict is the Portugal laurel, a very rare tree found along the streams in these mountains (route 16).

Other animals occur throughout the Iberian Peninsula, but never made it over the Pyrenees or the Alps. This is the case with most reptiles and amphibians. They are not confined to such a small area as the 'Lusitanian'

plants and animals, but nevertheless they occupy only a very small corner of the world. To give an impression of the uniqueness of this group, of the fifteen species of amphibians in Extremadura only five occur outside Mediterranean Spain, Portugal and France. Moreover, fifteen out of the twenty-three reptiles are confined to this region. Within Spain and Portugal, Extremadura is one of the most favourable areas, because it boasts a large number of creeks and rivers

The Spanish white broom (top) and the Spanish lupin (bottom) are both confined to the Iberian Peninsula.

and combines lowlands and mountains at short distances from each other. No wonder people interested in these animals hold Extremadura as one of their favourite destinations.

When it comes to more widespread species, the flora and fauna of Extremadura remain extraordinary because of its incredibly healthy populations of plants and animals found in small-scale agricultural landscapes. This is most pronounced when looking at the birdlife. The sheer number of serins, goldfinches, black redstarts, corn buntings, crested and wood larks, little owls, kites and others is amazing. Some other birds are uncommon or rare throughout most parts of Europe, but numerous up to the point of becoming mundane in Extremadura. Woodchat and southern grey shrikes, hoopoes, bee-eaters, griffon vultures, and booted and short-toed eagles simply show up everywhere in the lowlands of Extremadura.

The Portuguese laurel (top) is a rare relict of the cloud forests that covered Iberia in the warm and humid Tertiary period. It survives in the humid valleys of Sierra de las Villuercas, but is proper to the laurel forests of the Azores and Canary islands. The spiny greenweed* (bottom), a very common and conspicuous shrub, is typical for the Lusitanian distribution range (see following page for map).

FLORA AND FAUNA

88

Atlantic region

Heather
Calluna vulgaris
Mountain scrubland

Central European region

Alder
Alnus glutinosa
Mountain streams

Distribution ranges of widespread species

Flora and fauna of Extremadura is a multicultural society with plants and animals from many distribution ranges, which overlap in Extremadura. Some of the species are widespread (this page), while others are confined to a very small region (facing page). Most of the widespread species in Extremadura are truly Mediterranean, but there are also several with a distinctly central European and Atlantic distribution. Only a few come from tropical Africa.

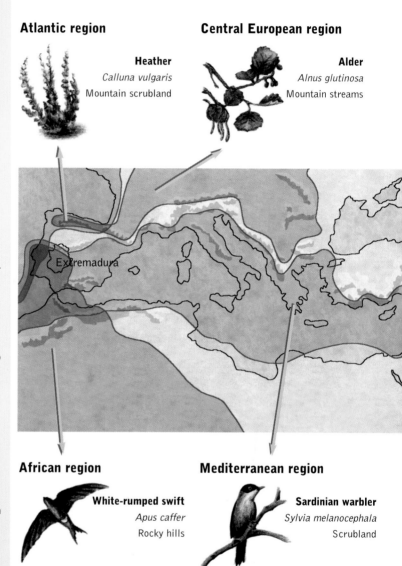

African region

White-rumped swift
Apus caffer
Rocky hills

Mediterranean region

Sardinian warbler
Sylvia melanocephala
Scrubland

Gredos region

Gredos' snapdragon*
Antirrhinum grossi
Rocky cliffs

Iberian region

Sharp-ribbed salamander
Pleurodeles watl
Lowland streams

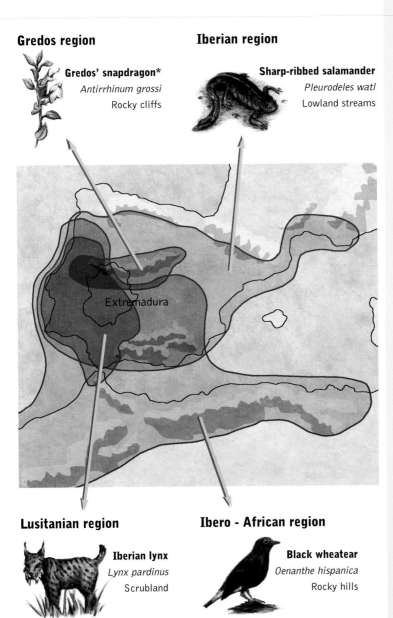

Extremadura

Lusitanian region

Iberian lynx
Lynx pardinus
Scrubland

Ibero - African region

Black wheatear
Oenanthe hispanica
Rocky hills

Distribution ranges of confined species

What makes Extremadura unique are the plants and animals that occur only in a very small region.
Four regions are typical for Extremadura. Iberia sometimes stretches into Mediterranean France. Southern Spain and north-Africa together form another distribution range.
The most unique species of Extremadura live either only in the Lusitanian region (southwestern Iberian lowlands), or in the Gredos Mountains.

Flora

If wildflowers are what you are interested in, the mountains should be your focal point. Along the routes in las Villuercas (routes 15 and 16) and the Garganta de los Infiernos (route 18) in the far north of Extremadura you may enjoy a very nice mountain flora. Furthermore, in Monfragüe (routes 1, 2, and 4) there are good numbers of interesting Mediterranean plants as well. Route 1, interesting primarily for ecology, birds and landscape, has a little detour into a small orchid paradise. The general dehesa flora, with its colourful display of short-living species, is very visible along route 5.

If technology permitted it, we would have placed a little chip on this page, right under the photograph of the gum cistus. The chip would have emitted the most typical smell of Extremadura: the sweet-herbal odour of *'la jara pringosa'*, the gum cistus. This most beautiful of all the cistuses can be found just about everywhere and is by far the most characteristic plant of the region, apart maybe from the western holm oak. In spring, when it opens its large white flowers, entire mountainsides look as if covered in a light snow.

The gum cistus is the most emblematic plant of Extremadura. The leaves and flower buds are sticky of an oily excretion that drenches the land in a wonderful sweet-herbal scent after a rain shower.

But in spite of its beauty and its wonderful smell, the abundance of the gum cistus signals a rather poor variety of plants. It is typically a plant of poor, acidic soils and is just as characteristic of Extremadura as it is for a species-poor vegetation. After fire, cutting or the abandonment of steppes and dehesas, the gum cistus can take over entire areas. Little grows under the cistus scrub, except the hypocist, a small parasitic flower that lives off the roots of the gum cistus.

Flora of the plains

The poor soils and rather monotonous bedrock make the plains of Extremadura, at first glance, not the most interesting place for plant enthusiasts. Even though Spanish scientists have recorded up to 45 species in a square metre of dehesa, these usually are not the most spectacular. The regular ploughing favours annual and biannual field and pasture plants, such as tolpis, purple viper's bugloss, andryala, corn marigold, Lusitanian spreading bellflower*, annual daisy and yellow chamomile. However, what these plants may lack in 'rarity', they make up for in numbers and thus in spectacular sights during the flowering season. In spring, dehesas turn yellow from different hawk's beard species and from tolpis, or white from annual daisy, chamomile and white asphodel. Purple also

has its place in this picturesque image. It is supplied by French lavender, galactitis, common stork's bill, purple sand-spurrey and purple viper's bugloss.

Between rocks and inedible shrubs, where plough and sheep's teeth do not reach, there are several more interesting plants to discover. Friar's cowl, which flowers in January, and pink foxglove* have found their niche on rocky ground and between the dog's teeth in the steppes (page 48). On grassier slopes, you can find tassel hyacinth, Italian gladiole, pink catchfly*, Iberian Jerusalem-sage*, narrow-leaved lupin, star-of-Bethlehem, tongue and sawfly orchids.

Pink foxgloves*, one of the many plants unique to the Iberian Peninsula, grow in clumps near rocks and tree trunks. Like the majority of the plants in Extremadura, it flowers in April and May.

Flowery meadow with
yellow chamomile.

Mountain plants

The mountains of Extremadura are like cool and moist islands in a
rather dry plain. Intercepting the lion's share of the rain-rich western
winds, the mountains boast a climate that is uncommon in the
Mediterranean.

Some vegetation therefore appears rather mundane to the average visitor from northern Europe. Silver birch occurs in a few isolated pockets
high in the mountains, alder trees desperately cling to the banks of permanent streams, and common juniper grows in the highest and coldest
regions of the mountains. In the herb layer, central European plants are
also numerous and include bastard balm, angular Solomon's-seal,
cowslip, narrow-leaved helleborine and early purple orchid.

Other plants, however, evolved on location and can never leave. Like the
boy in the bubble, they are imprisoned in their habitat by vast areas of
inhospitable terrain. Most of these species made it to the next mountain
range and maybe even to the one beyond that, but still they remain confined to the mountainous patches of Spain and Portugal. These plants
make the mountains of great botanical interest. Notable plants are the

Gredos snapdragon*, Heywood's foxglove*, Spanish lupin*, small-leaved milkwort*, red-flowered spurge*, pallid narcissus*, white flax, shrubby gromwell, Sicilian orchid* and Spanish adenocarpus*.
The beautiful western peony is unique to the Iberian Peninsula (p.65). It grows in the mountains and shady cork oak dehesas and is one of the highlights for botanists. The most emblematic plant of the Atlantic Mediterranean region must be the Spanish bluebell (p.64). It is common throughout the forests and scrublands of the mountains and the north-facing slopes of the lowlands.

While the mountains might form an island of suitable habitat for species that love coolness and moisture, the lowland flora finds itself in isolation as well (see page 85 for more details). Spiny greenweed* and tamujo*, widespread and common Extremaduran shrubs, can vouch for that. They are nowhere to be found outside southwestern Iberia. In rocky places you can find a local subspecies of dwarf sheep's-bit*, together with narrow-leaved cistus.
Most interesting are the spots with a soil that is a little different from the prevailing shallow, acidic bedrock. Often these are recognisable by being covered by cork oak dehesas. Here you can encounter the large Lusitanian milkvetch, palmate anemone, violet's birds-nest and several other plants that can also be found in the Mediterranean evergreen forest of Monfragüe.

Three beautiful species that mostly occur in the mountains. From left to right: Lusitanian milkvetch, small-leaved milkwort* and dwarf sheep's-bit.

FLORA AND FAUNA

Rockroses, brooms and heaths

Three plant families are particularly well-represented in Extremadura and, in fact, in the entire Mediterranean region. These are the rockroses, brooms and heaths. Together, they form the bulk of the scrubland plants. The family of rockroses is interesting because it evolved in the Mediterranean basin. Only a handful of species spread into other regions. Up until this day a hillside with flowering rockroses is as typical of the Mediterranean as a herd of wildebeest is of the African savannahs.

The rockrose shrubs give the scrublands their typical, flowery character. Their showiness makes them favourite garden plants in drier climates. The aforementioned gum cistus is the most common member of the family. It is often accompanied by the smaller sage-leaved cistus, which has pure-white flowers and oval leaves. Grey-leaved cistus is a bit similar, but has pink flowers. It favours the more calcareous soils and, being recognisable from afar, is a good indicator of spots where orchids and other limestone plants may grow. In dry, rocky places the narrow-leaved cistus grows. It is a small version of the sage-leaved cistus, only with linear leaves.

Other, more uncommon rockroses in the mountains of Extremadura are poplar-leaved, Portuguese* (within Extremadura confined to the Sierra de Gata), wrinkle-leaved* and laurel-leaved cistuses. The latter is typical of the Sierra de las Villuercas, just like the orache-leaved rockrose*, which has yellow flowers.

Like many broom species, the winged greenweed* is a plant favouring acidic bedrock.

The massive plant family of the peas, to which the brooms belong, is also well-represented in Extremadura. The Spanish white broom is one of the most common species and flowers between late February and early April. It is unique to the Iberian Peninsula and can turn entire hillsides white (p. 26-27). It is most common in areas with granite boulders. A little later, the yellow flowers of common broom appear. Retama puts up a more modest display between May and June. The small, greenish-yellow flowers cannot disguise the general scantiness of the retama scrub. Retama typically appears on the poorest soils, where management is minimal or has ceased. The spiny greenweed* is another shrub of these localities (p. 87). It is the most common of the nine species of greenweed in Extremadura.

Scrublands in the mountains are dominated by Spanish heath (top and middle), which is accompanied by umbel-flowered heath* (bottom).

The third plant family prominently present in the vegetation of Extremadura is the heath family. In general the heath family thrives in Extremadura because of the influences of the moist Atlantic winds. Heath scrublands are best developed on the poor soils in the mountains. Here Spanish heath prevails, together with bell-flowered* heath. Bordering the streams of the mountains is the white-flowering Portuguese heath, a tall species reaching up to three metres (p. 47). But the tallest family member grows in well-developed evergreen forests. It is the tree heath, which can make it up to five metres. It occupies a prominent place in the evergreen vegetation, just like another, rather odd member of the family, the strawberry tree (p. 139).

Strawberry trees have unique fruits that play an important ecological role as a food source for many birds and mammals. The ripe fruit contains alcohol. In the prime season, around November, it is not uncommon to see drunken foxes zigzagging on the roads of Monfragüe. People can eat the fruit as well, and it is not unsavoury. In Extremadura the fruits are used in cakes and sold in small quantities. Nevertheless, the name-giver of the plant recommends caution. Arbutus unedo, the scientific name, apparently means 'I only eat one'.

Bulbs

Building bulbs is the strategy par excellence for coping with the Mediterranean climate. If you were able to x-ray an average Extremaduran dehesa, you would be astonished at the amount of bulbs you would find. Technology doesn't allow this, but if it did, we wouldn't be surprised if 20 - 30% of the none-rocky soil were occupied by some form of onion. The bulb is such a great invention because it allows for the separation of an energy-consuming period (the flowering season) from an energy-supplying period (the leaf-bearing season). The leaves are usually out when temperatures and drought are not too extreme. The plant stores the energy in the bulb and when competition between flowers for insects is not too extreme, it produces flowers.

Large-flowered sand-crocus* form swaths of delicate pink over rocky soils in February.

Bulb flowers can therefore be seen at the oddest times. Many flower in autumn, like autumn squill, sea squill, autumn narcissus, autumn snowflake, Merendera and Portuguese autumn-crocus*.
Others appear in the dead of winter, like winter iris* and the rare, white-flowering Cantabrian narcissus*. But it is early spring that really smiles upon the bulb plant's life. While other plants need to start with their leaf growth before being able to make flowers, bulbous plants sprout with both leaf and flower at the same time. Around February and March clumps of bright-yellow hoop-petticoat narcissus and large-flowered sand crocus appear everywhere. Pallid narcissus* grows commonly on damp spots, occasionally accompanied by snakeshead and frequently by Spanish bluebell. Orchids -also bulbous plants- appear as well.

Hoop-petticoat daffodil is a common flower in the dehesa and in the Mediterranean evergreen forest.

Orchids

What applies to plants in general also goes for the wild orchids in Extremadura: there is a fair number of species, a few of which grow in good numbers, but most of them are rare and restricted to a few favoured spots. The highest diversity is found in a few isolated pockets in the mountains or in places with calcareous soil.

Generally speaking orchids are poor competitors. They are easily pushed out or overgrown by other plants. However, they stand their ground if the soil is too poor for grasses and more aggressive herbs to dominate. This would make the Extremadura a perfect place if it weren't for the fact that the acidity of the bedrock appeals to only very few species. The most common are tongue, lax-flowered, champagne and bug orchids, all of which occur in moister soils. Occasionally, they are joined by summer lady's-tresses, heart-flowered and long-lipped orchids. The small-flowered tongue orchid is hard to find, but not at all uncommon in the grassy dehesas.

Throughout the dehesas many other species emerge as soon as soils are not too acidic, such as pink butterfly orchids, milky orchids and sawfly orchids.

A little higher up in the mountains, on cool, humid spots in Mediterranean evergreen forests and cork oak dehesas, you may encounter violet bird's nest, dense-flowered orchid, Lange's orchid and green-winged orchid (subspecies *picta*).

Still higher up in the chestnut groves of the Sierra de Villuercas and La Vera you can find the beautiful flowers of Sicilian orchid, early-purple orchid and narrow-leaved helleborine.

Yet the very best places to head for are the few limestone hills that are present in the province (see plant hunting regions section on page 189). They suddenly boast a wealth of orchid species of the bee orchid genus, such as sawfly, mirror, yellow bee, woodcock, bee, sombre bee and Dyris* orchids. Much more conspicuous, however, are the giant and naked-man orchids.

Heart-flowered tongue orchid (left) near Alburquerque. Orchids of the mirror orchid genus are rather rare in Extremadura, because they prefer calcareous soils. Of them, the sawfly orchid (right) is the most widespread.

Extremadura's star is the green tongue orchid*. This orchid, which is confined to the small Extremaduran valley of the River Guadiana, is easily distinguishable, as it is the only non-red tongue orchid. Some experts, however, do not recognise it as a separate species, but as a variety of tongue orchid.

List of interesting plant species

Trees Quercus pyrenaica, Q. rotundifolia, Q. canariensis, Q. suber, Q. faginea, Alnus glutinosa, Castanea sativa, Prunus avium, Sorbus torminalis, S. latifolia, Fraxinus angustifolia, Taxus baccata, Betula pendula, Populus nigra, P. x canescens, T. tremula, Pinus pinea, P. pinaster, P. sylvestris.

Shrubs Prunus lusitanica, Cistus ladanifer, C. monspeliensis, C. albidus, C. salvifolius, C. crispus, C. laurifolius, Daphne gnidium, Pistacea lentiscus, Retama sphaerocarpa, , A. telonensis, Cytisus multiflorus, C. scoparius, Genista tridentata, G. hirsuta, Arbutus unedo, Viburnum tinus, Erica arborea, E. australis, E. lusitanica, E. umbellata, Calluna vulgaris, Thymus mastichina, T. zygis, Thymbra capitata, Quercus lusitanica, Q. coccifera, Rhamnus frangula, Pyrus bourgeana, Crataegus monogyna, Rosa canina, R. sempervirens, Rubus ulmifolius, Osyris alba, O. quadripartita.

Common conspicuous herbs Aristolochia paucinervis, Lupinus angustifolius, L. luteus, Astragalus lusitanicus, Anchusa azurea, Echium plantagineum, Orobanche rapum-genistae, O. ramosa, Phlomis lychnitis, Jasione montana, Campanula patula lusitanica, Campanula rapunculus, Umbilicus rupestris, Tolpis barbata, Galactitis tomentosa, Asphodelus albus, A. fistulosus, Urginea maritima, Scilla hispanica, Ornithogalum umbellatum, Muscari comosum, Leucojum autumnale, Narcissus serotinus, N. bulbocodium, N. fernandesii, Gladiolus illyricus, Gynandriris sisyrinchium, Arisarum vulgare, Tamus communis, Serapias lingua, S. parviflora, Asplenium petrarchae subsp. bivalens, Pteridium aquilinum, Cytinus hypocistis

Uncommon conspicuous herbs Euphorbia broteroi, Paeonia broteroi, Iris xiphium, Biarum arundanum, Ophrys dyris, O. tenthredinifera, O. bombyliflora, Cephalanthera rubra, Aceras antropophorum, Anacamptis pyramidalis, Orchis mascula, O. langei, O. olbiensis, O. coriophora, O. champagneuxii, O. papilionacea, O. italica and several other orchids Tulipa australis

Localised species (Iberian endemics) Lupinus hispanicus, Fritillaria lusitanica, Narcissus pallidulus, Polygala microphylla, Simethis planifolia, Drosophyllum lusitanicum, Digitalis heywoodii, D. thapsi, Anthirrhinum grosii, Serapias perezchiscanoi, Adenocarpus argyrophyllus

The oaks of Extremadura

Four species of oak dominate the forests and dehesas of Extremadura. Each of them has its own particular place in the landscape. Here is where they grow and how you can distinguish them:

The **holm oak** (top) is the tree of most lowland dehesas and of the low forests that cover rocky crests in the mountains. It has small, leathery, greyish-green leaves. The young leaves and those within reach of plant eaters are spiny. The older ones lack spines entirely.

The **cork oak** (also top) occupies the foothills and lowest slopes of the mountains, with rich soils. They grow taller than holm oaks and are of a deeper shade of green. The leaves are similarly shaped as the holm oak, but generally less spiny. The bark is the best way to distinguish cork from holm oaks (top right): cork oak has a deeply creviced bark of cork, whereas holm oak bark is smooth and hard.

Leaves of the holm and cork oak (top), the Portuguese oak (middle) and the Pyrenean oak (bottom).

The **Portuguese oak** (middle) is a large tree with fresh green, slightly lobed leaves and usually grows together with cork oak in moist regions with deep soils.

The **Pyrenean oak** (bottom) grows roughly between 600 and 1,800 metres and is originally the dominant tree of the Extremaduran mountains. It is easily distinguishable by the regular deep lobes in the leaves.

Mammals

Catching a glimpse of the rarer mammals of Extremadura is only reserved for those who are very lucky and very persevering. It is not something you should count on. Nevertheless, if you want to increase your chances from nearly zero to slightly better, Monfragüe (near Portilla del Tietar and surrounding dehesas, route 1) and Sierra de las Villuercas (the valleys of Navazuelas and Solana) are your best bets. Dawn and dusk are the times to be out. Don't get your hopes up for lynxes, but foxes, badgers, deer and boar are possible. With a little more luck, you'll get a glimpse of a genet or an otter.

Not that you will really notice much of it during your trip to Extremadura, but the mammalian wildlife of Extremadura is very rich and includes some extremely rare species, including the Iberian lynx, the Pyrenean desman and the Egyptian mongoose.

Most of the animals in Extremadura reside in the thick cover of mountain scrublands and forests. Here they find cover to hunt and shelter from being hunted. The dehesas attract larger herbivores such as red deer and wild boar. They are drawn by the pasture and, in the case of the boars, by the clearings, in which they can forage. In many dehesas the number of red deer is unnaturally high because they are bred for hunting purposes. The familiar roe deer of northern Europe is absent from Extremadura, except for in the Villuercas region. Roe deer occurr in the Mediterranean region only in isolated, well-vegetated mountain ranges. Game plays an important role in the food chain. Deer and wild boar eventually and inevitably go the way of all flesh, which for the larger animals in Extremadura coincides with the way of the vulture. Because game is less visible than cattle, it is often neglected as a food source for scavengers.

At one time wild boar and red deer had to fear the presence of the wolf as well. At the end of the 19th century, the province of Badajóz (southern Extremadura) was known as the best place in Spain to hunt wolves. At present, wolves are still fairly common in northwestern Spain, but in Extremadura they have been officially extinct since 1998, according to the University of Cáceres. The last count, in 1996, turned up five animals and no one would be surprised if wolves were spotted again at some point. In contrast to most of the other predators, which retreated into the mountains, wolves found their last refuge in the large cork oak dehesas in Sierra de San Pedro (between Cáceres and Badajóz). Here they dwelt in the large hunting estates and were not appreciated much by the owners.

FLORA AND FAUNA

The rabbit is a keystone dehesa animal, playing an important role in maintaining the dehesa ecosystem. It is the food it provides to other animals that makes it such a vital element. Rabbits have quite a reputation when it comes to appealing to the opposite sex, and the results of this are evident. Bunnies are in demand with Spanish imperial eagles and Iberian lynx, which have them as their bulk food. The importance of the rabbit became painfully clear when myxomatosis and RHD (two rabbit diseases) hit Spain and decimated the rabbit populations. Famine struck the Spanish imperial eagle and the population plummeted. (It probably did the same to the Iberian lynx, but that animal is so secretive that it is hard to tell.) Recognising that these two rabbit connoisseurs were already among the rarest animals in the world, you can imagine the blow this was to nature conservation.

The more open the dehesas become, the less mammals you will encounter. Apart from the occasional old fox and some mice, only the Iberian hare remains. Just like the central European hare, its Iberian colleague thrives in open grasslands and is a typical inhabitant of the steppes.

The most secretive animals live in trees, preferably in old ones, with lots of holes and cracks. This is where one of the fiercest predators of Extremadura resides: the genet. Genets look like a cross between a cat and a marten, with a long snout, a rounded back and a long, fluffy tail. It is strictly nocturnal and spends most of

The toilet of a genet: a masterly spot to defecate.

its time in trees, which is why it is so rarely seen. Dense dehesas with lots of old trees are the genet's perfect habitat. Genets have the nasty habit of silently creeping through the canopy at night and plucking sleeping birds from a branch. They also eat tree-dwelling lizards and garden dormice.

In the thick scrublands hide the other hunters: the badger, the fox, the wild cat, the Egyptian mongoose and the aforementioned Iberian lynx.

Mongoose originate from northern Africa and were introduced by the Moors. They are fierce snake-catchers. The Iberian lynx occurs, as far as is known, in the remote regions of Monfragüe, Sierra de Gata and Sierra de las Villuercas. It is very shy and secretive, has a large territory and hunts almost exclusively from the thick cover of the scrubland. This, plus the fact that the lynx is a beautiful and extremely threatened animal, generates the wildest and most exciting stories. Every now and then a park guard hears a cry or catches (or thinks he catches) a glimpse of a lynx at dusk in the more remote corners of Monfragüe. However, more reliable signs, like footprints or faeces, are rarely found. The Extremaduran government is planning to join the reintroduction program that has recently started in the Coto Doñana National Park in Andalusia. Hopefully, lynxes can be (re)introduced to Monfragüe within a few years.

Finally, the rivers and creeks of Extremadura support a healthy population of otters. The larger, more permanent streams have the most viable populations. In the mountain streams of Garganta de los Infiernos (route 18) the secretive Pyrenean desman occurs. The desman is an awkward creature, looking a bit like a mole with a vacuum cleaner's hose as a nose. In reality, its manoeuvrable trunk is a highly sophisticated tactile organ, much like an elephant's trunk. To the desman, sight is of no importance. It finds its food -aquatic invertebrates- solely by smell and touch. Because hardly anyone ever sees it, the desman tends to be forgotten. Yet it deserves more attention, because it is a unique animal that only inhabits the streams of the high mountains of central and northern Spain.

Two important mammals of the dehesa. The red deer (top) is kept for hunting, an important pillar for the maintenance of the dehesa landscape. The rabbit is bulk food for many predators, such as the Spanish imperial eagle.

Birds

Extremadura is a birdwatcher's paradise. Every route will offer the bird enthusiast a lot to see. Nevertheless, some routes are better than others. Monfragüe is top-notch, and then especially routes 1 and 2. The dehesa birdlife is richest along route 8, although any of the other dehesa routes will display the riches of its birdlife. Route 5 has some avian specialties, like Spanish sparrows and black-shouldered kites. The steppe birds can be easily seen along routes 10 and 12 (the latter is the very best route), but routes 8, 9 and 14 are also good candidates. Route 13 is interesting for rock-dwelling birds, as is route 15 and the aforementioned Monfragüe routes.

The saying goes that in Extremadura, whenever you look up, there is always a bird of prey cruising overhead, provided you have a clear view of a reasonable patch of the big blue sky. Optimists go even further and declare that such a patch always yields one raptor plus one griffon vulture. Repeated testing unfortunately proves otherwise, but the abundance of predators is so legendary that we maintain a slightly more modest saying: the Extremaduran sky always yields at least one raptor of some sort and often it is a griffon vulture or a black kite.

The black-shouldered kite uses wires and electricity posts as perch to hunt from.

Vultures

Monfragüe is the most renowned site for vultures. Over 400 pairs of griffon vultures, divided over numerous colonies, breed in this small nature park. Just about all other mountainous regions in the Extremadura, including the high altitude regions of la Vera, have their colonies of griffons.

The endangered black vulture breeds with more than 200 pairs in Monfragüe. They are even bigger than the griffon. With a wingspan of nearly three metres, they are the world's largest birds of prey, apart from the American condors. The third vulture is the much smaller Egyptian vulture. It is much less common than the previous two, because the competition with its larger relatives is too strong. The Egyptian vulture is left with the small bits and pieces of meat that the bills of the larger vultures cannot reach.

The reason for this high number of vultures lies both in the

Griffon vulture

land use and in the geology of Extremadura. The vast plains are the perfect scavenging ground. Thousands of cows, sheep, pigs, deer and wild boar graze in the extensive dehesas and steppes. The ability to cruise more than a hundred kilometres from the nesting site enables them to find most animal carcasses. Vultures soar to great heights, not only to spot the cadavers, but also to keep an eye on other vultures. As soon as one finds a cadaver and swoops down to check it out, the others soon follow.

Other birds of prey

Black and red kites, like vultures, are also definite scavengers. They scrape off everything that once lived and is now caked to the asphalt. Mice, snakes, ocelated lizards, toads and red-necked nightjars -in other words the most common roadkill- are the main food source for these birds. Red kites are very numerous in winter, when a large part of the central European population moves south to flee the cold and lack of prey. From March onwards, most reds disappear and are replaced by thousands of black kites. During spring and summer the black kite is the most numerous raptor in Extremadura, even outnumbering the griffon vulture.

The five species of eagle that occur in Extremadura are more into live prey. The most common ones are booted and short-toed eagles, both of which you are likely to see every now and then circling over the dehesas and lower mountains. The other three are the golden eagle, the Bonelli's eagle and the Spanish imperial eagle. These three are much more rare. Golden and Bonelli's eagles are largely confined to rocky mountain slopes. The Spanish Imperial eagle is a typical dehesa bird, breeding in large trees or occasionally on electricity posts and hunting for rabbits in the dehesas.

Black kites are Extremadura's most numerous bird of prey in spring and summer.

The lost family of the azure-winged magpie

There is something awkward about the azure-winged magpie. Within Europe, it is only found in the south-western part of Iberia, and here it is restricted to dehesas and other open forests. In Extremadura and parts of Andalusia and Portugal it is common, but that's it. Nowhere else in Europe will you see this sly and clever bird, and nowhere else in the world except... eastern Asia. Walk around in a city park in Beijing and there it is again -a little more drab-coloured, but that is more likely due to dust and exhaust fumes than to anything else.

Azure-winged magpies are rather shy animals, but on certain spots, such as at the Monfragüe camp site, they are fairly tame.

Iberia and then again East Asia. How is that possible?

There are two explanations for this strange disjunctive distribution. The first is that the azure-winged magpie once lived throughout Europe and Asia and disappeared everywhere except in the far eastern and the far western parts of its range. This seems an unsatisfactory explanation, because what would make the whole central part of this huge range suddenly unsuitable?

The second explanation is that the azure-winged magpie was brought from China by Portuguese travelers. This is also unlikely, because the birds seem so naturally adapted to a specific type of vegetation, namely the dehesas.

Molecular biology has provided an answer to this problem. A research group compared DNA from the Spanish and Chinese birds and it turned out that they were very different-so different in fact that the two populations are now officially declared two different species. Taking into account that this particular part of DNA evolves only very slowly, the difference was sufficient to make an estimate of the moment when the two populations separated: in the late Pleistocene, some 20,000 to 100,000 years ago. In other words, quite a bit before the Portuguese sailed back and forth between China and Portugal.

The Pleistocene period is well-known for its ice ages, which rudely shoved all life southwards. In the glacial ice age the climate was especially harsh. In its coldest period, the land ice reached all the way down to central Europe. The only areas in Europe and Asia that maintained a tolerable climate were the extreme southwest and the extreme southeast: roughly the areas which correspond with the present distribution of the azure-winged magpie.

Dehesa and steppe birds

The low-lying plains and low-altitude mountains of Extremadura are the most interesting areas for northern European birdwatchers. Here, the typical Mediterranean bird species can be found. Colourful birds, such as hoopoes, bee-eaters, woodchat shrikes and azure-winged magpies abound in the dehesas and steppes, whereas Sardinian and Dartford warblers are numerous in the scrublands beneath the holm oaks.

The vast treeless plains of Extremadura are home to the healthiest and most diverse population of steppe birds in all of Europe. Only two do not occur here: the Dupont's lark and the trumpeter finch. All the others are found in good numbers.

Corn buntings are ten-a-penny in the steppes and in the dehesas.

The contest for the title of most common bird of the steppes goes between the thekla lark, the calandra lark and the corn bunting. In our view the latter wins: in spring there is a corn bunting on every second pole. Stonechats, black-eared wheatears (the Mediterranean replacement of the northern wheatear), little owls, hoopoes, rollers, short-toed larks and southern grey shrikes are other typical birds of the arid grasslands.

Montagu's harriers and lesser kestrels are the resident birds of prey, frequently joined of course by their larger colleagues that glide in from nearby dehesas and mountains to hunt. Lesser kestrels breed in small colonies in abandoned sheds and barns. Like so many others, they have their mind set on the big crickets and locusts. The Montagu's harrier breeds on the ground in the grain fields and hunts for mice and lizards. Its majestic flight over the rolling dry pastures is a magnificent sight.

Another brilliant creature is the great spotted cuckoo. In contrast to Europe's common cuckoo, the great spotted belongs to a different, mainly tropical group of birds. But just like the common cuckoo it is a nest-parasite. The great spotted cuckoo targets magpies to do the job of child-rais-

ing for it (see text box on the following page).

A few birds have truly mastered life in the arid plains. These are the stone curlew, the bustards and the two sandgrouse.

The Stone curlew is the wading birds' odd man out. They never come to marshes, but prefer the dry grasslands, fields, semideserts and sandy dunes of southern Europe instead. Their saggy look and their large, sad-looking eyes make them a bit like the avian version of the homeless (p. 53). Their swollen joints give them their other English name: thick-knee. But despite their sorry look (and accompanying eerie cry) they are well at home under the scorching sun. Like many steppe birds they wait out the heat and become active in the evening.

The bustards are the kings of the empty lands. Although totally unrelated, they somewhat resemble the turkey. There are two species of bustard in Extremadura. Great bustards are -as the name implies- the largest steppe

The spotless starling lives in the same habitats as its relativr, the common starling in central Europe.

birds. The male is almost as tall as a stork, but with a more sturdy, bulky body. In groups they stride through the wavy high grass like the Spanish Armada on a breezy sea (they seem to float because their legs don't show in the high grass). The little bustard is much smaller, and in the breeding season it is highly territorial, with calling males all over the grassy steppes and scanty dehesas (see text box on following page). In spring they are fairly easy to spot. Apart from being such beautiful birds, both bustards are highly endangered throughout the areas in which they live, except in central Spain. The exact figure is unknown, but Extremadura,

Bee-eaters are easily the most exotic-looking birds in Extremadura.

Birds behaving oddly

Maybe it is the monotony of the landscape that instills a desperate need for excitement, but when it comes to mating, many steppe birds display rather extravagant behaviour. Here are five examples.

Great spotted cuckoos are bone-idle. The male and the female do not join forces to take care of their youngsters like proper parents, but are absolute team players in making sure other birds do.

The magpie is the victim, and knows it (the common magpie, not the azure-winged magpie). Whenever a magpie sees a great spotted cuckoo, it goes berserk. And magpies are team players too. If a cuckoo peeks into the nest, the diligent workers raise the alarm and chase away the intruder. The great spotted cuckoo knows that it will certainly taste defeat. So it nags and nags until the magpies are so annoyed that they chase him over the boundaries of their territories, and even beyond. Meanwhile, Mrs. great spotted cuckoo plants a single, great spotted egg.

Pin-tailed sandgrouse in a dry riverbed.

Sandgrouse are totally different. They are good parents. They show the young what seeds are edible and make sure they drink well. During the dry season the parents fly long distances to get water for their chicks. The adult bird uses its own breast feathers as a water bottle. With its precious cargo of water, the sandgrouse carefully flies back to the young to quench their thirst.

Preceding the stage of parenthood is the time of partner choice. The courtship of **little bustards** is odd, to say the least. The male stands on an elevated spot, raises its collar and sternly looks ahead. With a coolness usually reserved for cocks and wildfowl, it ludicrously serenades the unseen females with a softly croaking fart. It sounds like the kind that is inadvertently released during a sudden movement. The little bustard looks a bit disturbed while doing this, but if you thought it was an accident, just wait a few seconds for the bustard to draw back its head and, giving its head a sudden jerk, to produce another one. It seems a rather odd way of attracting a female, but, looking at the healthy population of little bustards in Extremadura, one can't deny the success of this courtship.

Male **great bustards** choose another way to impress the opposite sex: they blow up. If you watch the males carefully, you know when it will happen. They strut around majestically, checking out each other's potential. And then, in a split second, one of them blows up to a white feathery ball, like a grain of corn transforming into popcorn. What actually happens is that the animal rotates its feathers by 180°, turning up the white underside. This foam bath configuration, as it is sometimes called, can be upheld for several minutes.

Not nearly as silly is the romantic courtship of the **Montagu's harriers**. These aerial acrobats breed mostly in the cereal steppes and scout the area by flying low over the plains, suddenly turning and plunging down to surprise their prey. To confirm the bonds of matrimony the male offers its prey to its spouse. This is not done in a plain here-you-are-honey kind of way, but in a spectacular air show, in which the male flies up and drops the prey. The female catches it out of mid-air or grabs it from the male's claws. While doing so, she briefly turns around and flies upside down to welcome the gift. Courtship flights of Montagu's harriers just might be the most spectacular show of the Extremaduran steppes.

together with the plains of Madrid, Castilla-La Mancha and Castilla-Leon, probably supports over half of the world population of these birds. In contrast to the bustards, the black-bellied and the pin-tailed sandgrouse are highly elusive (p. 110). They stay close to the ground and are incredibly well-camouflaged. Sandgrouse are true desert birds. They live throughout the dry regions of central Asia, the Middle East, North Africa and Spain. Only in flight they are more easily spotted.

The mountains

After the steppes and the dehesas, the mountainous regions are the third birding hotspots. The rocky ridges of mountains like Monfragüe and Sierra de las Villuercas accommodate a number of beautiful and typically Mediterranean birds. This is where most big raptors breed, such as the Bonelli's eagle, the golden eagle, the Egyptian vulture and of course the colonies of griffons. This is also where black storks nest and where the enigmatic eagle owl retreats during the day.

Birds of smaller stature are present as well. Under the overhanging rocks the red-rumped swallow builds its igloo-shaped nest. The scanty shrubs sprouting from the rock cracks are the favoured habitat for rock buntings, black wheatears and the brilliantly coloured blue rock thrushes. The scrublands and little olive groves at the base of the mountains are good spots for finding melodious, Orphean and subalpine warblers, in addition to the more widespread Sardinian and Dartford warblers.

Cranes feed in the dehesa, but spend the night in large groups on the banks of reservoirs. The flight back and from the sleeping quarters are a spectacular sight.

Birds during the winter months

The most famous winter birds of Extremadura are cranes. These majestic birds mostly come from the Scandinavian countries, where they breed in bogs and swamps. They visit Extremadura between November and March and feed on the sweet acorns of the holm oak. When travelling through the dehesas in winter, you'll encounter small groups of them every now and then. Usually they are families consisting of two adults and one or two young. In the evening, these scattered groups take off and head for the nearest reservoir to spend the night.

The flight of the cranes to and from the reservoirs is an unforgettable sight. The best spots to witness this are given in the section on page 195.

Besides cranes, other northern and central European birds invade Extremadura in November, replacing the colourful spring and summer visitors. Red kites are the most numerous birds of prey during the winter months. Chiffchaffs enter the forests and dehesas. Thousands of wood pigeons and stock doves occupy the dehesas, pleasing predators such as peregrine falcons and Extremaduran hunters themselves. Song and mistle thrushes also become a common sight.

Cranes come to Extremadura in winter and feed on the acorns in the dehesas.

The steppes come to life as well. Thousands of lapwings, golden plovers, pipits and skylarks rummage about in the open fields. Rarer visitors are merlins and dotterels. Meanwhile, the permanent residents of the steppes huddle together in large flocks and keep a low profile, thus becoming much harder to spot than in spring. Mixed groups of thousands of larks and groups of house, Spanish and rock sparrows travel around like nomads in the desert.

Thus, although spring is the time when birds are most plentiful, the wintertime also offers a lot of interesting birds.

The top of the ticks

Of all the great birds of Extremadura, here are the top ten. These are the birds you should look for (the 'ticks' in birding jargon), because they are the most emblematic birds of Extremadura.

1. Black vulture The largest raptor of the old world once lived throughout southern Europe and the mountains of Asia, but has declined dramatically. The European population is estimated to comprise between 1,100 and 1,500 pairs, with over 1,000 living in Spain and around 250 in Monfragüe alone. The population size in Asia is not well-known.

2. Spanish Imperial eagle The world population of this beautiful eagle is estimated to amount to about 170 pairs, all of which breed in the western part of the Iberian Peninsula. This makes it one of the most endangered animals of the world. Around 40 pairs breed in Extremadura, almost a fourth of the world population.

3. Azure-winged magpie This inquisitive but shy bird wanders around in family groups in the dehesas. It only occurs in the southwestern part of the Iberian Peninsula. The Iberian population has recently obtained the status of a separate species, making it not only a typical but also a unique species for Extremadura.

4. Great bustard This huge bird holds the record for being the heaviest flying bird in the world. Spain holds over 50% of the world population. Together with the population near Villafáfila in northern Spain, the populations around Cáceres and Trujillo and in La Serena are the largest.

5. Black-bellied sandgrouse The Spanish population is the only one in Europe and the steppes of Extremadura harbour important populations. Black-bellied sandgrouse are, although hard to find, not uncommon in Extremadura. Outside Europe, black-bellied sandgrouse inhabit the flat uplands of southern Morocco and Algeria and from Turkey eastwards to Iran and the deserts of western China.

6. Lesser kestrel Nearly half of the world population of lesser kestrels lives in Spain. The largest colonies are located in the towns of Cáceres and Trujillo, with numerous small colonies in old barns in the surrounding steppes.

7. Black-shouldered kite This beautiful, small raptor with enigmatic red eyes is common throughout most parts of Africa and southern Asia. It invaded Spain in 1975. Today it lives in the southwestern region of the Iberian Peninsula.

8. Little bustard The smaller cousin of the great bustard used to be common in large parts of southern Europe, but today just small populations in Italy and southern France and some large populations in Spain have survived. Again Extremadura is the region with the largest community. Elsewhere in the world, only the steppes of Kazakhstan and southern Russia may have healthy populations.

9. Pin-tailed sandgrouse Except for La Crau, a small nature reserve near the Camarque in France, the Spanish population of pin-tailed sandgrouse is the only one in Europe. The pin-tailed is less common than the black-bellied in Extremadura. It lives in more desert-like environments in the lowlands.
Outside Europe, the pin-tailed sandgrouse is a widespread but generally rare bird found at the edges of deserts in North Africa and the Middle East.

10. Griffon vulture Although not uncommon in the rest of Spain and several other regions of southern Europe, the density of griffon vulture reaches its peak in Extremadura. These huge birds are simply everywhere and are the most emblematic birds of Extremadura.

Except for the mating season, the males of the great bustard retreat to their own gentlemen's societies and stay away from the females.

FLORA AND FAUNA

Reptiles and amphibians

Finding reptiles and amphibians is not so much a case of where but of when. Amphibians are most easily found on rainy or cloudy evenings in autumn, winter and spring. The easiest way is to drive along the minor roads while carefully checking what pops up in front of your headlights. An evening stroll with a flashlight along any of the streams will also turn up many amphibians.

Reptiles are plentiful during warm weather but seem absent when it is cold. Stonewalls are the classic localities for the more common species of lizards. The steppes are usually a rewarding place, but the lower mountain ranges have more diversity. See also section 'finding amphibians' on page 191.

When it comes to finding reptiles and amphibians, Extremadura is once more the place to be. The picturesque streams, with their ribbons of water crowsfoot, are full of loudly croaking Perez's frogs (the Spanish counterpart of the central European water frogs), while stripeless tree frogs crawl around in the adjacent bushes. Stripe-necked terrapins sit on the rocks bordering the creek, enjoying the warmth of the sun, while small viperine snakes rush around in the water, chasing after the schools of tadpoles. Extremadura has it all and that is because it is both warm and has a fair amount of creeks, pools and rivers, satisfying the needs of both the cold-blooded and the moisture-dependent creatures.

The false smooth snake is usually active at night and can be found in evenings in dry, rocky terrain.

The Mediterranean sun is sufficiently warm for the cold-blooded lizards and snakes to support a year-round activity. During the cool win-

The Almonte river (top) harbours many species of amphibi-ans, such as the Iberian midwife toad (inset).

ter days rocks are used as sun-bathing spots to warm up for the day. Many reptiles in Extremadura remain active while reptiles in central Europe are in deep hibernation (winter sleep).

In contrast to central European amphibians, the amphibians in the low-lands of Extremadura have swapped seasons entirely. In summer, when water becomes scarce, they hide underground and wait for the colder and moister months to become active. After the rains in October and November, they come out and leave for their mating pools. If you go out on any of the minor roads in the dehesas on a moist November evening, your headlights will catch frogs and newts crossing the streets.

The creeks, pools and streams harbour no less than eleven species of frogs and toads and four species of newts and salamanders (see list on page 121). Among them is the prehistoric-looking sharp-ribbed salamander. It is the largest of the European amphibians, reaching up to 30 centimetres, or the size of a normal ruler. The sharp-ribbed salamander is very well adapted to the Mediterranean drought. It cannot stand the fierce sun directly, but is a skilful refugee. It buries itself deep in the soil and can stay there for a long time. In this way, the sharp-ribbed salamander can even survive in the dry steppes, where it lives in small, temporary pools or in the ground when the pools have dried out.

The Iberian midwife toad and the Western spadefoot are similarly flexible adaptors, living in the driest of regions and hiding underneath stones and in the ground during the dry season.

The viperine snake is a common water snake and the biggest enemy of all aquatic life, including the rare frogs and newts. Together with the stripe-necked terrapin, the viperine snake represents the reptiles in the Extremaduran creeks and rivers. Stripe-necked terrapins are very common in any type of pond or creek, regardless of the quality of the water. Its cousin, the European pond terrapin, is rare, only occurring in the few reedy marshlands of the region.

Away from the creeks and into the dry dehesas and steppes of the low-

The marbled newt

lands, the diversity of reptiles increases. Lizards are the most conspicuous reptiles, rushing out in front of you when you walk along stonewalls or in scrubland. The most common species on walls is the Iberian wall lizard, which looks deceptively similar to the 'normal' wall lizard that does not occur in Extremadura.

The most conspicuous scrubland reptile is the large psammodromus: a plain, olive-coloured lizard with two bright stripes along its body (p. 177). The Spanish psammodromus is smaller and lives in more open terrain. It is a little less common and a much shier animal, making it difficult to spot. Another small lizard of open terrain is the spiny-footed lizard. All three scrubland lizards are confined to the Iberian Peninsula, except the Spanish psammodromus, which has a few populations along the French Mediterranean coast.

So now from the little lizards to the big one. The ocellated lizard is an impressive beast, reaching up to 80 cm. Occasionally, even larger specimens have been found. This really is a choice piece of lizard for the reptile-

eating short-toed eagle to come home with. The ocellated lizard is Europe's largest normal lizard and lives in holes in the ground. It is common in the drier dehesas and steppes, but to find it you'll have to be aware of sudden movements in the grass. They are very agile and during warm weather they dash across the road with such speed that you are left wondering whether you actually saw one or just thought you did.

Ocellated lizards are hard to spot, but snakes are even worse. Except for the little viperine snake, the other seven are highly elusive. Again, the short-toed eagle is to blame for this, together with its snake-hunting colleagues. Snakes are often thought of as top predators, but in reality they only take up a very modest middle position in the food chain. They hunt for rodents, young birds, lizards and frogs, but are hunted by short-toed and booted eagles, mongoose, genets and storks. The young snakes even have to watch out for any type of mid-sized bird, so they cannot be too cautious.

Different lizards occur in different habitats. The Iberian rock lizard (top) inhabits the highest and coldest regions of the Gredos Mountains, while the Spanish psammodromus (bottom) favours the hottest, most sun-soaked lowlands.

Six snake species occur in the dry dehesas, steppes and rocky mountain slopes. The largest is the fierce Montpellier snake, which reaches up to two metres in length. It climbs into trees to hunt for eggs and young birds and is the most common snake in Extremadura, together with the ladder and viperine snakes. Ladder snakes also inhabit Extremadura's dry steppes and wastelands.

To prevent being hunted, the false and the southern smooth snake go out at night. During the day, they hide underneath stones, only to come out when the sun comes close to the horizon. They start off by warming them-

A rare picture of a unique animal: the worm lizard, a worm-like reptile that lives underground and hardly ever surfaces.

selves on the rocks and the asphalt before going off to hunt. Needless to say that the late hours of the day are the best time to spot them.

The oddest creature of Extremadura is perhaps the worm lizard. It looks like a giant shiny earthworm (up to 30 cms). And that is basically what it is, except that it is a reptile. It seems headless. Worm lizards are almost strictly subterranean, only coming out of the ground in heavy rains or at night. Other reptiles in Extremadura are three-toed and Bedriaga's skinks and Moorish and Turkish geckos. The geckos live in houses, sheds, stone walls and creviced cork oaks. The Moorish gecko is the most common one, often seen running over the walls of houses on warm evenings. They love to hunt for insects around streetlights. Watching Moorish geckos dashing around on a warm evening on a terrace with a glass of wine in your hand is just about the best holiday feeling the Mediterranean has to offer.

Moving from the lowlands up into the mountains, the geckos soon leave the scene. In fact, the reptile and amphibian world changes almost completely. The colder climate suddenly makes a winter slumber justified again and the summertime less of a problem for the moisture-dependent amphibians. The aforementioned reptiles and amphibians become rare (except for the large psammodromus) and are replaced by central European species like the midwife toad and the fire salamander (the Iberian 'Almanzor' subspecies). The reptile diversity is also lower in the mountains, but there are two rare and beautiful creatures that occur only here. The first is the Schreiber's green lizard (see cover), the most colourful of the Iberian lizards. The males have sky-blue throats and almost neon-green backs. They live around mountain creeks and can be spotted sunbathing on rocks in spring. Higher up, when nearly all reptiles have thrown in the towel because of the cold, the Iberian rock lizard takes over. It is extremely cold-resistant and lives in rocky fields above the tree line.

List of reptiles and amphibians of Extremadura

Aquatic environments viperine snake, grass snake (r), Schreiber's green lizard (in mountains), European pond terrapin (r), stripe-necked terrapin, southern marbled newt, Bosca's newt, sharp-ribbed salamander, fire salamander (only in mountains), Iberian midwife toad, midwife toad (r), Iberian painted frog, Iberian parsley frog, Iberian frog (r), Perez's frog, western spadefoot

Scrubland, steppes, dehesas, temporary pools Montpellier snake, horseshoe whip snake, ladder snake, ocellated lizard, spiny-footed lizard, Spanish psammodromus, large psammodromus, three-toed skink, Bedriaga's skink, slow worm (r), worm lizard, southern marbled newt, sharp-ribbed salamander, Iberian midwife toad, common toad, natterjack toad, western spadefoot, treefrog, stripeless treefrog

Rocky habitats southern smooth snake, false smooth snake, Lataste's viper, Iberian wall lizard, Iberian rock lizard (only high up in the Gredos), ocellated lizard, spiny-footed lizard, Spanish psammodromus, large psammodromus, worm lizard, Turkish gecko (r), natterjack toad

Urban environments
Turkish gecko (r), Moorish gecko, Iberian wall lizard, common toad

Insects and other invertebrates

Dry-land invertebrates, such as yellow scorpions, scolopendras, tarantulas and praying mantises are common in all stony lowlands, but are especially numerous in the steppes (routes 8 and 12 are the best). The butterfly fauna is remarkably rich in species, but to appreciate this, one needs to go up into the mountains (routes 15, 16, 17, but above all route 18). For the latter, a visit in May-June is recommended.

Birdwatchers have Extremadura high on their lists and so have nature enthusiasts focusing on reptiles, amphibians and plants, but entomologists (people interested in invertebrates) rarely make it to Extremadura. This is probably because most of the interesting species, primarily butterflies, fly around in the mountains, rather than in the plains. Whereas the high mountains of Spain such as the Cordillera Baetica in Andalusia, the Pyrenees and the Sistema Central have a lot to offer, the number of butterfly species in the mese-

tas and Extremaduran lowlands is limited. The most numerous butterflies are small coppers, Spanish marbled whites, green-striped whites and Moroccan orange-tips. The caterpillars of these species feed on grasses, docks and short-lived flowers, which is probably why they are numerous in Extremadura. However, other invertebrates are very common in the plains. In fact, the invertebrate wildlife of Extremadura is -at least to the northern European- a very exciting and exotic world, with many large and odd-looking creatures to be found in every

Spanish yellow scorpion (top), Scolopendra (middle) and Scutigera* (bottom). They represent the seamy side of steppe life, residing under stones, rocks and holes in the ground. They come out at night to hunt; you won't find them unless you go out to look for them. The sting / bite of the first two can be dangerous.

nook and cranny. Grasshoppers become very conspicuous towards the summer months. In the steppes they have often formed plagues, carpeting entire fields and ruining entire harvests. Of the many species of grasshoppers, the one to blame for this behaviour is the Moroccan locust. It is a medium-sized grasshopper, recognisable by four white lines forming a cross on its back (thorax). Today, the locusts are held at bay through the careful application of insecticides (see also page 54).

Towards the summer, the chirping of crickets and red cicadas reaches its peak. The sound, together with the dead yellow grass and paralyzing heat, forms the face of the Extremaduran summer. This is also the time for finding pray-ing mantises. These extraordinary large insects spend their time in high grass and bushes, where they are not uncommon, only extremely well-camouflaged. They hunt for grasshoppers, butterflies and other insects. Two eye-catching species are the common praying mantis and the hooded praying mantis*. The latter is brown and has a strange, pointed 'Egyptian hat' (p. 54).

Praying mantises form a group of mostly tropical insects. Only a few species make it into Europe. Next to praying mantises, there are more 'tropical' invertebrates to be found in Extremadura. If you head for the steppes or lowland dehesas, you can marvel or shiver at the sight of scorpions, giant centipedes, tarantulas and other creatures that are usually considered to belong to the seamy side of nature. Fortunately for people who dislike them, they can only be found by those wishing to find them (see page 190 for search tips).

The red-striped oil beetle has very short wing cases, which gives it the appearance of a worm rather than a beetle.

Only the somewhat repulsive-looking red-striped oil-beetle comes out into the open. This beetle has very short wing-cases, giving it the appearance of a giant black and red maggot on stumpy legs.

In the second half of spring and early summer, when the grassy and bushy mountain slopes burst into flower, the butterfly enthusiast can indulge him or herself in searching for butterflies in the mountains of Extremadura. Most species in the mountains are no stranger to central Europe either. Most numerous are scarce coppers, brimstones and Camberwell beauties. Piedmont ringlet is a typical mountain butterfly, which you may also encounter in the Alps.

Two-tailed pasha (top), Spanish festoon (middle) and southern white admiral (bottom) are three stunning butterflies proper to the Mediterranean forest.

Only a couple of species have a more restricted Mediterranean or western distribution, like the beautiful Spanish festoon, the two-tailed pasha and the southern white admiral. The first two are typical for the Mediterranean forest because the caterpillars feed on plants that grow mostly here. For the Spanish festoon this is the green-flowered birthwort* (p. 141), while the two-tailed pasha's caterpillar is on a strict diet of strawberry trees (p. 139). The butterflies grace the flowery slopes at the base of the mountains.

Moroccan orangetips are quite common in April and May.

Some butterflies of Extremadura

Central European species *(mostly in Gredos mountains)* Camberwell beauty, small-pearl-bordered fritillary, large wall brown, pearly heath, scarce copper, mazarine blue, brimstone, olive skipper, silver-washed fritillary, dark green fritillary, silver-studded blue, ilex hairstreak, small copper, swallowtail, scarce swallowtail, large turtoiseshell, silver-spotted skipper, Niobe fritillary

Southwestern and mountain species *(mostly in Extremaduran mountains)* Piedmont ringlet, black satyr, meadow fritillary, dusky heath, Esper's marbled white, mountain argus

Mediterranean species *(mostly in evergreen forest and lush dehesa)* Spanish Festoon, two-tailed pasha, southern white admiral, green-striped white, cardinal, Spanish marbled white, and Moroccan orange-tip, cleopatra, nettle-tree butterfly, Spanish purple hairstreak, Lang's short-tailed blue, yellow-banded skipper (only spot in Spain is western Gredos mountains)

THE PRACTICAL PART

In the following part of the guide we recommend routes that are particularly suited for seeing the great many specialties of the area. Furthermore, from page 188 onwards we provide practical information and observation tips for visitors to Extremadura. This information comes with two warnings. First, remember that things change: campsites may go bankrupt, books and maps may be sold out, and birdwatching hotspots may change. Second, we are not claiming to be complete in our listings of the things to do, establishments to stay at, and so on. We just offer our experiences by way of helpful suggestion. Our recommendations are not based on any universal standards (if there are any), but just on our own preferences. You'll have to find out for yourself whether our judgment agrees with yours.

Suggested routes

All itineraries described on the following pages are numbered. The numbers are shown on the general map in the back flap of this guidebook.
The time indication of the routes is based on very leisurely excursions with lots of stops. The itineraries are straightforward, but have been written to be used together with a map of the area (see section 'maps' on page 190).
If you are pressed for time, we suggest you concentrate on the surroundings of Torrejón el Rubio, Trujillo and nearby Monfragüe (for example routes 1, 2, and 8). A short visit to either La Vera (routes 17 and 18) or Sierra de Villuercas (routes 15 and 16) can be added for the sake of completeness.
For a more thorough exploration we suggest to reserve between ten days and two weeks.

Hiking the Garganta de los Infiernos (route 18).

Route 1: Monfragüe NP round trip

FULL DAY OR MORE

Diverse drive along rivers and creeks; through the scrub-covered mountains of Monfragüe splendid cork and holm oak dehesas.
Maybe the very best Extremadura has to offer, not only for birdwatchers but for anyone with an interest in nature.
More vultures than you can count and many, many more birds.

Habitats on this route: dehesa (p 25); creeks, rivers and reservoirs (p 42); Mediterranean evergreen forest (p. 56); the mountains (p. 62).

This beautiful, long trip leads straight through the Monfragüe nature reserve and the surrounding dehesas. Along the way, spectacular sites and rarely visited hotspots alternate, all of them yielding interesting plants, animals and beautiful scenery. There are some larger stops with possibilities for short strolls. Some spots are worth visiting a second or third time, because this route is quite a lot for one single day.

In summer, the Arroyo de la Vid has reduced to a string of pools.

Departure point Torrejón el Rubio

From Torrejón go north in the direction of Plasencia.

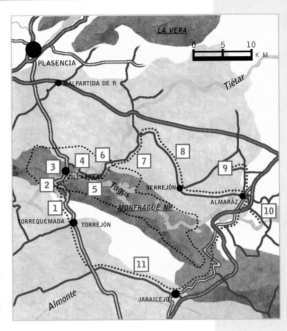

1 Hardly out of Torrejón, you are already surrounded by the fine holm oak dehesas that are so typical of Extremadura. Drive slowly and allow yourself a good look around, for the avian treasures can pop up anytime. In spring you will probably see and hear hoopoes, azure-winged magpies, bee-eaters, corn buntings, crested larks, wood-chat shrikes and with luck a Spanish or rock sparrow. Spanish Imperial eagles breed in the area and are sometimes seen hunting here.

The holm oak dehesa extends to the Corchuelas mountain range that marks the beginning of the Monfragüe nature reserve. Halfway between Torrejón and Monfragüe, the road descends into the valley of the creek 'Arroyo de la Vid'. This is a good spot to stop and walk around a bit. The rugged slopes are a bit bushier than the surrounding dehesas and support Sardinian warblers. In late March you can search for pallid narcissus and milky orchid in the scrub. Further upriver, in the steep part of the valley, black storks, eagle owls and Egyptian vultures breed. Occasionally, they fly by.

Continue along the road until you reach the edge of the Tagus reservoir and encounter a car park on your left hand side. A little further is another one closer to the rocks.

2 You are now at Monfragüe's front door: the Peñafalcon or Salto del Gitano. This is the famous vulture rock, without a doubt the most famous tourist spot in Extremadura. The Salto del Gitano is an impressive breach of the Tagus river through the Sierra de las Corchuelas. There are a number of interesting things here.

The face of the rock on the other side of the river harbours a big colony of griffon vultures, sometimes accompanied by a pair of peregrine falcons, blue rock thrushes or Egyptian vultures. Black storks breed in the fissures just above the water line. To see their nest you have to walk a little further, go around the curve and then look back to the rock. Once the air starts to warm up in the morning the vultures depart on their carrion raids and sometimes soar right over your head. Keep an eye open for black vultures, which do not breed on the rocks themselves but in the nearby north-facing slopes of the Sierra.

On the rocky pinnacle beside the road and the rocky outcrop on your right you can find rock buntings, red-rumped swallows and blue rock thrushes. Botanists will find this spot interesting too: on the rocks to the right grows the Spanish adenocarpus*, an endemic broom-like bush of the mountains of southwestern Spain. Next to the road grows the pink foxglove*, a plant endemic to Spain and common in Extremadura.

Continue along the road along the northern slope of the mountain range and cross the massive bridge over the Tagus River. Proceed along the winding road for another two kilometres until you reach the hamlet of Villarreal de San Carlos a little off the road to your right. Park here for coffee and an exhibition.

3 Villarreal is the only settlement in the park and therefore its centre. At first glance there is not much that is 'royal' to detect in Villarreal (which means village of the king). However, the village, consisting of one street, was founded by King Carlos III to house royal guards, who had to ensure the safety of the travellers in this rough, desolate terrain full of robbers.

The Peñafalcon is Monfragüe's dramatic entrance. From the side of the road you can watch the vultures on the cliff.

Continue further along the road and, after a kilometre, turn right in the direction of Saltos de Torrejón.

4 The rather barren hills with French lavender and gum cistus you are now traversing are not directly the most interesting part of the park from an ecological point of view. On the contrary, the hills are a silent witness to the times during which the park was formed and Extremaduran nature conservation was born. These hills were planted with rows of eucalyptus as a resource for the paper industry, just like all of Monfragüe would have been if it weren't for the efforts of a number of Spanish nature conservationists. The eucalyptus has been removed and the first colonisers, French lavender and gum cistus, are slowly invading the barren ground.

Black storks breed on cliffs along the rivers of Monfragüe.

5 Just before reaching the dam in the Tiétar River there is a bird observation hut to the right: the Mirador la Tejadilla. It overlooks a small colony of griffon vultures on the rocky slope on the other side of the river. Sometimes the Egyptian vulture is present too. It is not the most exciting spot and cannot compete either with the Peñafalcon you visited on your way into the park or with the Portilla del Tietar, which is still to come.

Cross the dam and continue through the pine plantation and over the hill until you join the Tiétar river on your left hand side. Stop at the picnic spot on your left hand side just before a little bridge and proceed on foot.

6 A few hundred metres ahead you see another rocky outcrop on the other side of the river. This is the Portilla del Tiétar, Monfragüe's more modest but still very scenic back door. As often with back doors, this site is actually more interesting than the front. At the Portilla del Tiétar,

THE PRACTICAL PART

there is also a colony of griffon vultures. Although this one is smaller, you can get closer than at Peñafalcon. The Portilla itself and the surrounding cork oaks and rock crevices harbour a changing assemblage of breeding birds, such as booted, short-toed and Spanish imperial eagles, Egyptian and black vultures and black storks. It used to be a classic site for eagle owls, but they recently traded places with a nest of Spanish imperial eagles. When you visit the area in spring, just ask somebody with a telescope and you'll know exactly what breeds at the site that year. Golden eagles regularly pay a visit from Monfragüe's more remote mountain ranges. Other nice birds are blue rock thrush and red-rumped swallow. With luck you might even see otters in the river.

Continuing on foot beyond the actual Portilla brings you to a small but beautiful and dense Mediterranean evergreen forest with strawberry trees, tree heath, laurustinus and cork oaks. In early spring the delicate pallid narcissus flowers. A bit further the evergreen forest gives way to a beautiful old and dense cork oak dehesa and, to top it off, a restaurant on your left hand side. The entire walk is only about two km (back and forth).

Walk back to the car and continue along the road.

7 A little ahead you pass through an old dehesa-like landscape with narrow-leaved ash. On your right, you come across a dirt track with a bike route to Serrejón. It leads through a mixed holm and cork oak dehesa, which you can enter. There is less fencing here, meaning there is some freedom to wander around. It is a perfect spot for a stroll or picnic in the dehesas.

The northwestern part of Monfragüe was once covered with eucalyptus plantations. They were removed and the original vegetation is allowed to recolonise the barren hills.

Follow the road again and turn right towards Serrejón.

8 This new road leads through extensive holm oak dehesas. Closer to Serrejón are a few calcareous outcrops with an interesting flora (including wild tulip and dyris orchid*). But there is more of this further on.

Continue towards Almaráz. In Almaráz you pass the nuclear plant. Although these parts are less scenic, there are two interesting sites in the area.

9 The first spot of interest is a little north of Almaráz. Follow the road towards Saucedilla. After about two kilometres you pass the edge of a reservoir, from where you can scan the open waters of the Embalse de Arrocampo for ducks, grebes and, in winter, cormorants. In Saucedilla, turn left. This route leads past the northern edge of the reservoir. Here are extensive reedbeds with some -for Extremadura- very rare birds like purple herons, purple gallinules, marsh harriers and Savi's warblers. The meadows in the area are also good for observing the ever-elusive black-shouldered kite.

10 The second spot is of interest for plant enthusiasts. From Almaráz follow the very small road towards Valdecañas de Tajo. Right on the other side of the highway, there is a hill with olive groves on your left hand side. This hill is a limestone outcrop, which is rare in Extremadura. Along the small trails between the olive groves you can find a wealth of orchids in April, including mirror orchid, dyris orchid*, yellow bee orchid, sawfly orchid, giant orchid, naked man orchid and small-flowered tongue orchid.

Shrubby germander is one of the flowery shrubs that make the Mediterranean evergreen forest attractive. It grows near the Portilla del Tiétar.

Return to Almaráz and follow the road south to Casas de Miravete and further on to Jaraicejo. Traffic on this rather broad road is now very light because of the highway that was build right next to it. For visitors, this makes it a pleasant drive, with ample possibilities to stop along the way to take in the wide, desolate landscape and scan the dehesas. These parts are very good for raptors, which breed in large numbers in the nearby strict reserve part of Monfragüe.

From Jaraicejo, turn right towards Torrejón el Rubio.

11 Again dehesas. This stretch has very old, stumpy holm oaks. Along the way there are several bee-eater colonies quite close to the road. The very last stretch of dehesa before hitting the Trujillo-Torrejón road is very scenic in April for its masses of flowering French lavender.

Turn right to Torrejón. If you made all the stops along this route, it must be midnight by now.

In some dehesas between Jaraicejo and Torrejón French lavender flowers abundantly.

Route 2: The castle of Monfragüe

135

6 HOURS
MODERATE

Splendid landscape of dense forest, sheer rock cliffs and wide views over endless dehesas.
One of Iberia's most intact Mediterranean evergreen forests and its botanical treasures.
Black and griffon vultures at arm's length

Habitats on this route: dehesa (p. 25); Mediterranean evergreen forest (p. 56); the mountains (p. 62).

This is the classic Monfragüe hiking trail, leading you past all of the major sites of the nature park save two, and is almost obligatory for first-time visitors. This trip, a part of the 'red route', combines some rather touristy spots, such as the castle and the Peñafalcon (the vulture rock), with more extensive and tranquil hiking.

Departure point Torrejón el Rubio

Getting there Leave Torrejón in the direction Plasencia / Monfragüe. After about 10 kilometres the castle of Monfragüe comes in sight on your right. There is a parking spot at the right hand side of the road at the base of the Sierra de Corchuelas (see map). This is the departure point.

From the car park, walk (rather than drive) up the track towards the castle.

1 The walk up leads you through the *solana* (south-facing) slope of the mountain. In comparison to the dehesas of the plains, it is covered with a more dense vegetation. A mixture of holm and cork oak, wild olive and Mediterranean hackberry covers the hill, lavishly decorated with the colourful shrubs of spiny greenweed*, thyme and French lavender.
Although the southern slope is more vegetated than the dehesas, it is no match for the *umbría* or shady northern slope, as you will see on your descent from the other side of the mountain.

THE PRACTICAL PART

2 On the last stretch up to the castle you are treated with an increasingly beautiful view of the extensive dehesas of Extremadura. The cliffs to your left have some shallow caves with rock paintings from the Neolithic age.
Check the rocks for blue rock thrushes, rock buntings and crag martins. With some luck, you will encounter a black wheatear. In June the extremely rare and essentially African white-rumped swift is sometimes seen here.
After a few wet days, when little pools have formed on the track, you are treated to a nice extra. Little flocks of house martins, crag martins and red-rumped swallows gather mud to build their nests. The crag martins and red-rumped swallows nest in nearby crevices in the rocks.

Upon reaching the castle, enter the tower and go up the uneven stairs to the top. Here you can sit and have a break on top of the thick outer walls.

3 From the castle you have stunning views over both the north and south facing slopes of the sierra and a breathtaking vista of the dehesas (p. 28). We found this an excellent spot to rest and have breakfast. A

The view from Monfragüe castle over the north slopes of the mountains. Blue rock thrushes often sing from the castle ruins.

constant stream of griffon vultures pass by above you, below you and at eye-level, occasionally alternated with a black vulture. The vultures use the warm air rising over the south slope of the mountains to glide by and to gain altitude. On the castle ruins there is usually a pair of blue rock thrushes present as well.

Next to the tower, a small trail leads down the northern slope. The trail is recognisable by a small stone arch.

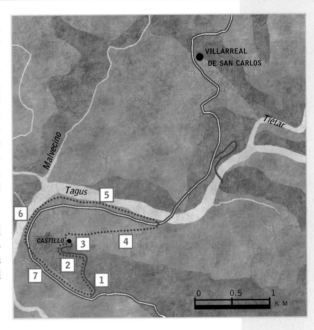

4 Almost immediately after you go down the trail the atmosphere becomes cooler and moister. Rocks are heavily overgrown with moss and Mediterranean selaginella. The birdlife looses its Mediterranean touch and consists largely of blackcaps, chaffinch blackbirds and robins.
The first part of your descent is steep, followed by a stretch of nearly level walking. This is where you enter the real evergreen forest. The plant species you encounter are strawberry tree, tree heath, laurustinus, false olive, turpentine tree, holm, cork and Lusitanean oak, Montpellier maple and wild jasmine. On the forest floor you should look out for Lange's and dense-flowered orchids, palmate anemone and green-flowered birthwort*. In summer, the beautiful two-tailed Pasha (one of the most beautiful butterflies in Europe) can be found here (p. 122).

Just before reaching the end of the trail, another trail departs to the right. This one is described in this guide as route 3, but can easily be used as an extension of the present route. If you choose to walk it, read on at point 3 of route 3. If not, continue further down, until you reach the Fuente del Frances. The spring is situated right next to the big bridge over the Tagus river. At mornings and evenings, when people have deserted the spot, the songbirds of the *umbría* come down to the spring to drink.
From the spring go further down to the river (on the right side of the bridge) and follow the trail that goes underneath it.

5 The narrow and sometimes tricky track is situated in the little strip between the road and the river in such a way that the road is hardly noticeable. The track beats walking over the road, but does not have very much to offer. The vegetation offers more of the *umbría* plants and occasionally you might see a Spanish festoon (butterfly) fly by. In clearings it pays to scan the sky for vultures, eagles and black storks.

6 The trail rejoins the road just before the Peñafalcon. The last few metres offer you a splendid sight of the vulture rock, right on the spot with the best view of the black stork nest at the base of the rock. For the full description of the Peñafalcon, see route 1, point 2.

7 The last bit of the trail is a little over 1 kilometre and needs to be covered using the paved road. It leads through some nice holm oak dehesas.

Additional remarks Avoid doing this route on weekends and holidays, especially in spring. Furthermore, it pays to start early. Not only to beat the crowds and to have the view all to yourself, but also because in the morning the vultures departing on their carrion raids need the warm air over the *solana* to gain altitude. Therefore, they follow the mountain range and soar by very close to the castle. The swallows and martins on the track (see point 1) leave when the crowds arrive.
If you do not feel like walking long stretches, this route can be broken down into several small parts. The castle can almost be reached by car by driving beyond the parking place, the Peñafalcon can be admired from the road itself and there is a parking spot near the Tagus bridge, from where you can walk a few minutes to get a taste of the Mediterranean forest.

Route 3: Two sides of the Tagus

3½ HOURS, MODERATE

Lovely and rather quiet walk through the lushest part of the *umbría*.
Very lush vegetation of Mediterranean evergreen forest.

Habitats on this route: creeks, rivers and reservoirs (p. 42); Mediterranean evergreen forest (p. 56).

This short loop, part of the 'red route', forms an elegant and rather quiet hike. It lacks smashing sites like the Monfragüe castle, the Peñafalcon and the Portilla del Tiétar, but in return offers a more tranquil exploration of the most beautiful part of the Mediterranean hardwood forests and of more open terrain, interesting for the smaller Mediterranean birds.

Fruits and flowers of the strawberry tree. The red berries are edible and form an important food source for birds in winter.

THE PRACTICAL PART

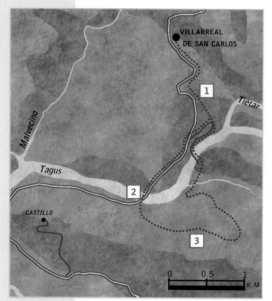

Getting there From Torrejón, go north in the direction of Plasencia. Aproximately 1.5 km after crossing the Tagus river, turn right towards Villarreal de San Carlos, which lies just beside the road.

From Villarreal, walk down the only street past the herdsmen huts (built in herdsmen style, but meant for visiting groups), and go down to the Tagus river.

1 The walk down leads through a very open area. It follows the old road from the original Puente Cardenal bridge towards the village. This is also a part of the old *Cañada Trujillana*, one of the big transhumance drover roads. This hillside is hot and sun-soaked. The slope faces southwards and has a slate surface with French lavender sticking out here and there. This is a good spot to search for reptiles, butterflies and rock-dwelling birds, such as rock bunting, blue rock thrush and black wheatear. In the air, just about any raptor can turn up. In some years this is a good area to look for Bonelli's eagles.

When you are near the river, you come across a small, paved road. Turn right and follow this road up to the main road. Turn left and head for the main bridge.

2 From the bridge you have a good view over the deep Tagus valley. Apart from the hundreds of nests of house martins under the bridge, this is also a good spot to search for alpine swifts, especially during mornings and evenings. In winter, look out for rock sparrows on the parapet. Look to the left to see if the much lower 'Puente Cardinal' surfaces. This is the original bridge, which today spends much of its time under water. Only if the water in the reservoir is low can it be used. If it is passable, the Puente Cardenal will be incorporated into your way back.

3 After the bridge, turn left and follow the small trail up the mountain, towards Castillo de Monfragüe. After about 5 minutes the trail splits. Take the left branch, signposted 'casa camineros'.

The first section is a steep ascent through a dense and luxuriant evergreen forest. The *umbría* effect (see page 56) on the shadow side couldn't be any clearer on this route: the hot, rock-covered slope you have just left behind makes way for big, green laurustinus trees and strawberry trees.

After an initial strenuous climb, the trail smoothens and runs straight east. Look out for violet bird's-nest (a big, purple orchid) and dense-flowered orchids (tiny and insignificant) under the tree heath and strawberry trees. In summer, keep an eye open for the two-tailed pasha (a butterfly; p. 122). Its caterpillars feed on the leaves of strawberry trees.

A little further on you come to a vantage point overlooking the forest, river and hillside you just traversed.

From here onwards you start to descend again. The trail brings you to the Fuente de la Parra, a well with three basins, richly decorated with bramble

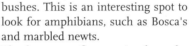

bushes. This is an interesting spot to look for amphibians, such as Bosca's and marbled newts.

The last part of your trip along the *umbría* side runs through more open terrain with gum cistus, French lavender and, in early spring, lots of flowering Lusitanian milkvetch. Check this area for Dartford, Sardinian and subalpine warblers.

Once on the small paved road bordering the river, turn right in case it is possible to cross the Puente Cardenal. The road leads over the bridge. On the other side you can pick up the trail from which you came down in the beginning of the walk and head back to Villarreal de San Carlos.

If the Puente Cardenal cannot be traversed, turn left to the main bridge, cross it and follow the road back to Villarreal.

The green-flowered birthwort* is the larval food plant of the Spanish festoon butterfly.

THE PRACTICAL PART

142

Route 4: Cerro Gimio and the Malvecino creek

3½ HOURS
EASY-MODERATE

Diverse and quiet walk through scrubland, riverine and umbria forests.
Interesting flora harbouring both an abundance of typical and a number of rare species.

Habitats on this route: creeks, rivers and reservoirs (p. 42); Mediterranean evergreen forest (p. 56).

In comparison to all the dramatic landscapes and vulture colonies of Monfragüe, the more modest-looking route along the Malvecino creek is somewhat underrated. This is for the better, as it means that it is less visited and therefore well-suited for a more relaxed exploration of Monfragüe. The final destination of this route, the Cerro Gimio mountaintop, nevertheless treats you to the fabulous views you might by now expect from an excursion in Extremadura. Along the route (marked as the green route) you can enjoy an interesting flora and a nice birdlife.

Departure point Torrejón el Rubio

Getting there From Torrejón, go north in the direction of Plasencia. Approximately 1.5 km after crossing the Tagus river, turn right towards Villarreal de San Carlos, which lies just besides the road.
From here walk some 50 metres along the road in the direction of Plasencia and where the road bends to the right, take the dirt track departing to the left.

Wild tulip, one of the rare wild flowers that grows along this trail.

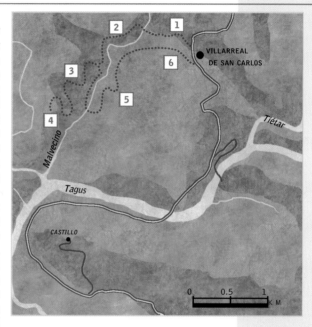

1 The track leads gently downwards. On your left-hand side you see a nice scrubland, but on the right the scenery is bleak: an empty hill with small bushes and bare rock. This is the part of Monfragüe Natural Park that was cleared and replanted with Eucalyptus as part of the reforestation plan to supply resources for the paper industry. Fortunately, this plan was thwarted by the nature conservationists. Several years ago, all Eucalyptus trees were removed and today these bleak hills are the reminder of what could have been the fate of all of Monfragüe. Now the land is left for the cistus and lavender shrubs to recolonise the hills. In the meantime it has become a good stretch to find lizards, like Spanish and large psammodromuses and Bedriaga's skinks.

Once downhill, the trail crosses the Malvecino creek and bends left to follow it downstream.

2 Streams like this one greatly contribute to the natural splendour of Monfragüe. It usually carries water throughout the year and is therefore of vital importance as a water supply for mammals like wild boar and red deer.

In the grassy borders of the creek quite a number of wildflowers grow. Most species commonly found in Extremadura are found together, like star-of-Bethlehem, pink catchfly*, rosy garlic, tolpis, Lusitanian bellflower, star clover, tassel hyacinth, spotted rockrose, brown bluebell and pink foxglove*. If you visit the region in spring, this and the following sections of this walk form a good place to introduce yourself to the Extremaduran flora.

THE PRACTICAL PART

144

When the creek bends to the left, the route follows and both enter a steep-sloped valley, where the trail is shaded by holm oaks. Further on, the trail splits, and to get to Cerro Gimio you have to follow the right branch.

3 The trail towards the summit of Cerro Gimio leaves the holm oak forest and enters a dense scrubland of gum cistus and Spanish heath. Keep an eye open for raptors and black storks, which often pass by from nearby breeding spots.

4 Continue along the green route until you reach the top of the Cerro Gimio mountain. From here you have a marvellous view over the Tagus, the castle of Monfragüe and the Salto del Gitano, the breach of the Tagus through the low Corchuelas mountain range. The rock face on the right side of the Tagus is the Peñafalcon vulture rock. Closer by, you see the Arroyo Malvecino flow into the Tagus. On the right another creek, the Arroyo Barbaón, also pours out into the river. The shores of these creeks are favoured fishing spots for black storks. The Cerro Gimio is also a good place to spot the ever-elusive Bonelli's eagle and peregrine falcon, although luck still has to be on your side to find them.

A little current pouring in the Malvecino creek. It only carries water after abundant rainfall.

Go back to the Arroyo Malvecino and cross it.

5 On the other side of the creek the trail follows the creek upstream again. You have now entered a young Mediterranean evergreen forest consisting largely of holm oak, but with an a mixture of tree heath, strawberry tree and laurustinus. In the grassy patches pallid narcissus*, green-flowered birthwort*, Spanish bluebell, palmate anemone and southern daisy are frequent.

6 When you are nearly back in Villarreal, wildflower enthusiasts are treated to two very interesting plants: Spanish fritillaria and wild tulip. You can find them along the last stretch of scrubland before entering the deserted meadows of Villarreal. In the moist meadows a little further on grow common and small-flowered tongue orchids.

The Malvecino creek in winter.

Route 5: The olive groves between Monroy and Talaván

2 HOURS
EASY

Smashing display of flowers in spring.
Umbrella pines with characteristic white stork colony and hundreds of subletting Spanish sparrows.

Habitats on this route: dehesa (p. 25).

The stretch between Monroy and Talaván forms a gap in the dehesa landscape. It forms a quilt of small parcels of olive groves, pastures, meadows, scrubland and 'dehesa-ish' groups of holm oaks. A number of tracks lead through this area and all are worth exploring.

Although the area cannot qualify as a proper dehesa, the diverse landscape supports many of the typical plants and animals of dehesas, such as hoopoes, azure-winged magpies and woodchat shrikes. Furthermore, it is a good place to find booted eagles and, with luck, black-shouldered kites.

Departure point Torrejon el Rubio

Getting there Head in the direction of Cáceres. Just after kilometre post 34.5, a dirt track branches off to the right. You can park at the side of the road and walk up this track.

Take the first right and immediately turn left again and walk on. Further ahead, the trail turns sharply to the right but a branch continues straight ahead. Follow the latter until it reaches another track. Turn left here and follow it until it reaches the road (ignore the other branch to the right).

1 The nice thing about olive groves is that they do not serve as grazing ground for cattle, so there is no need to fence them off. You can walk freely over the trails without worrying about property owners.

Along the entire track you will be treated to a smashing display of colour coming from hundred of thousands of wild flowers. They are mainly short-living species that profit from the recently ploughed or sowed fields, such as small-flowered and pink catchflies*, purple viper's bugloss, large blue alkanet, et cetera. Between the olives and holm oaks the ground turns yellow with the flowers of yellow chamomile. Tassel hyacinth is also very common and in a few

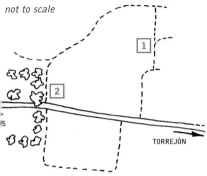

spots there are groups of the beautiful champagne orchid. On patches of scrubland French lavender, spiny greenweed*, gum and sage-leaved cistuses flower exuberantly in spring. Black kites, booted eagles and sometimes black-shouldered kites hunt the open terrain. The latter species is always hard to find, because it turns up in different areas each year. Where there are mice -usually near cereal fields- the black-shouldered kite is sure to follow.

2 Upon reaching the road you see a group of the distinctive umbrella pines on which several storks have built their nests. In the branches of the nests and in the trees itself, hundreds of Spanish sparrows have built their own nests, and the noise of their chirping overrules the clattering of the storks.
In the moist meadows and the roadside before the pines you can find hundreds of tongue orchids flowering in April.

Cross the road and follow the dirt track. Take the first left and then again turn left on the first occasion. When you reach the road turn right; after 50 metres you are back at the departure point.

The landscape between Monroy and Talaván.

Route 6: The Ermita of Talaván

3 HOURS
EASY

Walk through dehesas and scrublands that are so typical of the lowlands of Extremadura, including its wildlife.

Habitats on this route: dehesa (p. 25); creeks, rivers and reservoirs (p. 42).

The walk to the chapel (ermita) of Talaván is not the type of route on which you should expect top-notch habitats or birds. Rather, the interest lies in its connection to the landscape and nature associated with dehesas and Extremaduran rural life as it is present behind fences and stonewalls all over Extremadura. The track down to the chapel does not cross private property and can therefore be entered freely.

Departure point Talaván

Getting there The trail starts at the northern (and low) end of the village. Enter the village and proceed to the Plaza de los Herradores. Continue over calle de las Amapolas, plaza Ramon y Cajal, and finally the calle de las Margaritas. At the end there is an open spot amidst walled parcels. A wooden information panel at the end marks this place. Here the route starts.

Take the trail to the right.

Ancient walls flank the first part of the route, just outside the village. These walls serve as fences for rather small parcels of land. The trail is part of the old vereda -the side road of the great cañada (see page 76). Originally, the vereda crossed the Tagus, but since the river has been been dammed, the trail ends at the water's edge. Along the trail you find masses of barbary nuts in spring.
Continue along the main track, ignoring a sidetrack to the left and later a side track to a farm, also on your left hand side.
Past the farm the parcels are more sizable. The dehesas around you are covered with a thick undergrowth of gum cistus. The birdlife is dominated by bee-eaters, hoopoes, Sardinian warblers, woodchat shrikes, azure-winged magpies, booted eagles and black kites (and reds in winter).

Near the river the trail runs steeply down the slope of the Tagus valley. From here you have a splendid view over the Tagus reservoir, the dehesas on the far side of the river and the mountains in the background. The vegetation around the track is much denser, which is typical of those steep river valley slopes, where cattle are not able to browse as freely as in the plains.

At the end of this route you encounter the newly built ermita (chapel) de Talaván. It is a place of contemplation and the residence of the Holy Virgin, patron of the village of Talaván. During the annual pilgrimage, the people of Talaván go to the chapel to worship (each village has its own chapel; the people of Torrejón for example, have theirs in the castle of Monfragüe).

The old chapel of Talaván has disappeared under water: one of many victims of the river dams. When water levels are low, you can see the chimney of the old chapel appear from the water on the opposite side of the

river. In ancient days the people of Talaván used to fish in the river and during the pilgrimage (*romeria* in Spanish) little boats would bring the villagers over.

Return along the same track.

Additional remarks
The steppes between Talaván, Santiago and south to Cáceres host many steppe birds, including a fair amount of rollers (on the electricity posts). A tour over the minor roads, although not described as a route in this book, is just as beautiful as any other tour over minor roads.

The track towards the Ermita of Talaván.

Just south of Talaván lies the embalse de Talaván, a small reservoir, which can be overlooked from the road between Talaván and Cáceres. In winter about 2,000 cranes come to roost in the reservoir and fly over the aforementioned road at dusk. There is a small car park next to the reservoir, from which you can observe the cranes.

Route 7: The Torrejón reservoirs

1-2½ HOURS
EASY

Nice track for a quiet evening stroll.
Some interesting birds.

Habitats on this route: dehesa (p. 25); creeks, rivers and reservoirs (p. 42).

This trip is perfect for taking in the evening air on a relaxed post-dinner stroll, but is not worth spending a whole day on. The track connects several estates and ends at the gate of a private terrain. Along the way you traverse holm oak dehesas and crop fields.

Departure point Torrejón el Rubio

Standing in the main street of Torrejón and facing north, take the first street right after the Monfragüe pension. Follow the narrow street all the way to the end of the village, where you stumble upon a small reservoir that is the water supply of the village.

1 The small Torrejón reservoir is worth checking for waterfowl. Often there is not much more than a grey heron and a great crested grebe, but one never knows. At dusk, just before it gets dark, red-necked nightjars appear and hunt over the water and bordering dehesa. They are easily recognisable by their odd, far-carrying and continuous *ka-TOK, ka-TOK* sound. In winter and spring, the reservoir is a good location for finding southern marbled newts, sharp-ribbed salamanders, natterjacks and Iberian midwife toads.

The track passes the reservoir on the northern side and continues through the dehesas for about four kilometres until it reaches a second, larger reservoir, where it ends.

2 Along the trail you are treated to the typical dehesa nature. The spring flora includes Iberian Jerusalem sage*, Italian gladiole, galactitis, champagne and tongue orchids.
The edges of the open fields, about halfway down the track, are interest-

map is not to scale

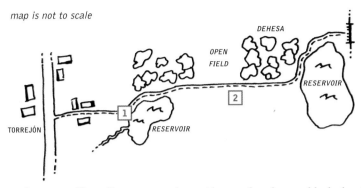

ing because of breeding stone curlews. About a decade ago, black-shouldered kites also prospered here, but they seem to be gone now. Still, this is the terrain they prefer, so it pays to keep an eye open.

The way back is the same as the way up.

Additional remark Another option for an evening excursion is to follow the track past the cement factory and into the dehesas. The cement factory is on the western edge of the village. Along the small creek, amphibians are plentiful in autumn and winter.

Woodchat shrike

152

Route 8: The plains between Trujillo and Cáceres

FULL DAY OR LONGER

Great birdwatching with rarities of dehesas, steppes, towns and cultivated areas.
A most diverse landscape with all the best of the lowlands of Extremadura.

Habitats on this route: dehesa (p. 25); creeks, rivers and reservoirs (p. 42); steppes (p. 48).

This is the route to take for anyone wanting to experience the great plains of Extremadura. Endless fields and steppes alternate with expanses of dehesa, intersected with steep river gorges and the enchanting stony landscape of the granite boulders. Both as a scenic drive and as a birdwatching trip, this route is guaranteed to impress.

Departure point Trujillo

Getting there Leave the town on the northern side in the direction of Torrejón el Rubio and Plasencia. After 5 kilometres, turn left towards Monroy.

1 This minor road leads you through some excellent steppes and dehesas. The first part is studded with massive granite boulders. In early spring the shallow soil turns pink with stork's bill. This is also the best time to find great spotted cuckoos, which are quite common in this stony landscape. Little owls, little bustards, lesser kestrels, hoopoes and lesser grey shrikes are also present in generous supply.
A little further ahead, the landscape becomes flat and open. This is a good area to find calandra larks, stone curlews, Montagu's harriers and little bustards. In recently ploughed fields, keep an eye open for black-bellied sandgrouse.

Turn left towards Sta. Marta de Magasca.

2 The first part of this road leads through grain steppes again, which have a birdlife similar to the stretch you have already passed. Further ahead, the steppes make way for dehesas, right before the gorge of the Sta. Marta creek. The transition zone between steppes and dehesas is worth a quick stop, because

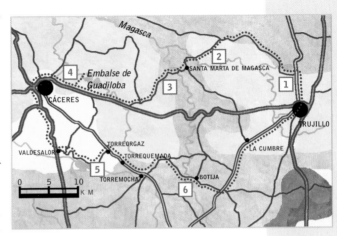

this zone has a large number of little bustards in spring. The banks of the Sta. Marta creek form a good stop for a picnic. In the creek you can find stripe-necked terrapins and viperine snakes, while the shrubby dehesas bordering the creek are interesting for warblers.

Continue along the road to Sta. Marta. In the village turn right (not signposted).

3 Outside Sta. Marta the road descends into another river gorge (equally suitable for a stop) and then climbs up again. The dehesas once more make way for open plains. These plains, however, form the edge of the great Llanos de Cáceres, one of the largest centres in Spain for steppe birds, such as great bustards. With some luck you will be able to find them, although here they are more difficult to spot than near Trujillo (route 10) or in La Serena (route 12). Just about all other steppe birds can be encountered here as well. Especially numerous are lesser kestrels and Montagu's harriers. In early spring, great spotted cuckoos sit on the electricity wires (always a good spot to keep an eye on). Storks come in to hunt from Cáceres. In short, if you came for birdwatching, this is a place to drive along slowly and to keep your eyes open.

The road ends on the main Trujillo - Cáceres road. However tempting, do not stop to watch birds here, because you are bound to get into a car accident. For an interesting extra excursion, take the exit after the gas station, signposted Embalse de Guadiloba.

THE PRACTICAL PART

The Arroyo de
Magasca

4 The big reservoir 'Embalse de Guadiloba' is situated close to Cáceres and right in the heartland of the Llanos de Cáceres steppes. On the far side of the reservoir (around which you can walk) you can often spot great bustards. You can try your luck for black-bellied sandgrouse and collared pratincoles in the ploughed fields between the main road and the reservoir. In any case, a small walk on the trail around the reservoir is a good way of getting a closer look at the steppes that you have so far only been able to watch from the car.

Back on the road, continue to Cáceres (UNESCO site and home to one of the largest colonies of lesser kestrels in Spain) and carry on towards Mérida. Follow the road until you reach the village of Valdesalor. Here turn left towards the Embalse de Salor and Torreorgaz. At the time of writing the road towards Mérida was being converted into a highway. Therefore the exact traffic situation is unknown, but the Embalse de Salor -also a popular picnic spot for people from Cáceres- can certainly be reached from the Valdesalor village.

5 The Embalse de Valdesalor is a small reservoir in a landscape of granite boulders and bordered by Eucalyptus trees. The surrounding fields are lush and green and full of hunting storks from nearby Cáceres. The area around the reservoir is perfect for spotting black and red kites (the latter in winter), booted eagles, southern grey shrikes, little owls and great spotted cuckoos. In spring, the road is lined with tassel hyacinth and hoop-petticoat daffodils. Also keep an eye open for black-shouldered kites, which are seen here every now and then.

From Torreorgaz, turn right towards Torrequemada and Torremocha. At Torremocha, turn right towards Botija.

6 The small country road towards Botija and Torremocha leads through fields, pastures and dehesas. Near the bridge crossing the Tamuja River (just before Botija) is a nice bee-eater colony.

When the road reaches the Trujillo - Montanchez road, turn left. Nineteen kilometres further ahead you are back in Trujillo.

Additional remarks This trip is rather long. For a thorough exploration of all the points of interest, including a visit to the towns of Cáceres and Trujillo, you will need two days.
This trip is also perfect as a two-day trip by bike, provided that you leave well-prepared.

Griffon vultures resting after a meal. In the background another dozen or so fly by.

THE PRACTICAL PART

ROUTE 9: LOS BARRUECOS

Route 9: Los Barruecos

2-3 HOURS
EASY

Impressive granite boulder landscape, with a colony of white storks breeding on top of the boulders.

Habitats on this route: steppes (p. 48).

Just west of Cáceres, the small nature reserve of los Barruecos (319 hectares) comprises an odd and intriguing landscape with ponds and gently rolling hills with huge granite boulders. Some of them are the size of a church. Los Barruecos also offers a good opportunity to stroll around in the Cáceres lowlands without hitting upon fences all the time. Along this route you will encounter a typical flora and fauna of the arid grasslands and scrublands of Extremadura, but the real treat is a big white stork colony on the top of the boulders. It is the only spot in Spain where storks breed on the ground.

Departure point Cáceres

Getting there Follow the direction of Malpartida de Cáceres and Valencia de Alcántara. In Malpartida de Cáceres, turn left at the sign 'Los Barruecos'. Follow it until you reach the reserve and a small car park on your right. There are three way-marked trails in the area, ranging from a half-hour pit stop to a three-hour walk. The routes are well signposted and straight-

Granite boulders dominate the landscape of Los Barruecos.

forward. From the restaurant, follow the trail along the lake to the large boulders ahead with the storks on them.

1 The lake is artificial, originally created for washing wool. It is rich in amphibians and is a good spot to find viperine snakes. In winter the lakes are frequented by several species of duck, such as wigeons, teals and red-crested pochards. In spring you will find black-winged stilts, little grebes, little egrets and cattle egrets around. During warm weather you can find the pretty spiny-footed lizards running around in the open terrain, while the scrub of Mediterranean mezereon and Spanish white broom hides the large and Spanish psammodromuses (two species of lizards).

If you visit los Barruecos in the early morning, you might find little owls, hoopoes and southern grey shrikes perched on the rocks. In the surrounding fields little bustards, stone curlews and Montagu's harriers occur.

White storks hunting for frogs in the shallow waters of the reservoir.

THE PRACTICAL PART

Route 10: The steppes of Belén

2 HOURS

Very good trip for finding steppe birds, such as little and great bustards.

Habitats on this route: steppes (p. 48).

The steppes of Belén are one of those need-to-know spots, where it is ridiculously easy to find steppe birds, especially the much sought-after great and little bustards. This trip is so short that if you leave early enough, you can have seen great and little bustards and be back in time for breakfast on the Plaza major in Trujillo. Another advantage of this route is that the birds are not as easily disturbed as in other spots in the Plains of Cáceres and Trujillo.

Granite boulders near Trujillo. In early spring the ground is covered with common stork's bill.

Departure point Trujillo

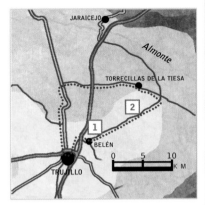

Getting there Follow the signs towards the Madrid-Badajóz highway and turn right, signposted Belén. The village of Belén is just on the other side of the highway. Go through the village and follow the only road on the other side of it.

1 The first few kilometres lead through hills with big granite boulders, small bushes and stonewalls. There are many magpies here, making it an excellent spot to find great spotted cuckoos, which places its eggs exclusively in magpie nests (see text box on page 107). This small-scale landscape is also favoured by hoopoes, lesser grey shrikes and little owls. The latter often sit on the stonewalls and boulders, but look treacherously like stones themselves.

2 A little further ahead the steppes stretch out in front of you like a wild-west terrain. If you are here in spring, stop along the road at good vantage points to scan the grasslands with your binoculars. It shouldn't take long to discover the typical call of the little bustard. Further in the fields you should be able to find some great bustards. Closer to the road, calandra larks and stonechats are numerous. Stone curlews and both sandgrouse also occur in the area. Later in the day, when the air has warmed, vultures fly overhead. Black vultures in particular seem to favour these parts. After a few kilometres there is a mixed stork and cattle egret colony in a dead tree on your left-hand side.

At the end of the road, turn left towards Torrecillas de la Tiesa (there are bug orchids along the road in May). Go through the village and continue through some fine holm oak dehesas until you reach the Torrejón-Trujillo road again. Turn left, back towards Trujillo.

Additional remarks For suggestions on how to find birds in the steppes, see page 193.

Route 11: The mountains of Montánchez

3 HOURS
EASY-MODERATE

Interesting intermediate terrain between mountain and lowland.

Bulbous plants and Mediterranean warblers galore.

Habitats on this route: the mountains (p. 62).

The Sierra de Montánchez is a low mountain range in central Extremadura. It is one of the typical mountain islands in the rolling lowlands of Cáceres and Trujillo, from which you have a splendid view over the surroundings. Several nice walks depart from the picturesque village of Montánchez, of which the 'blue route' is described below.
The walk leads through olive groves, scrublands, Pyrenean oak forests and chestnut groves, habitats typical of the medium-sized mountains of Extremadura. However, the Montánchez mountains lack the spectacular scenery, flora and fauna of La Vera and Sierra de Las Villuercas. Therefore, we think this route is best recommended if you are not planning a visit to those other mountains.

Departure point Montánchez

The trail starts right from the Plaza de los Toros in Montánchez village and follows the blue markings. The blue route departs together with the red one and largely follows the same track.

The first section of the trail is enclosed by stonewalls where, on warm days, Spanish wall lizards and large psammodromuses appear from the cracks. A little further ahead you enter a chestnut grove full of rosy garlic, tassel hyacinth, Spanish bluebell, star-of-bethlehem and the occasional early purple orchid. Late in spring the giant fennel flowers make for a spectacular sight.
At the end of the grove the red route splits off to the right and the blue route continues through an open landscape with olive groves and scrubland consisting of Pyrenean oak, bracken fern and Spanish white broom. Alongside the trail the pink flowering wrinkle-leaved cistus* and the white

sage-leaved cistus flower in spring. Sardinian warblers and rufous nightingales are common, but keep an eye open too for Dartford, Orphean and subalpine warblers. Behind the terraced mountain slope you have nice views over the endless, dehesa-clad lowlands.

The trail turns left around the mountain and climbs up a little to the mountain top, which is also the highest point of the Sierra de Montánchez. The upper slope is clad with Spanish white broom. The trail now crosses the mountain and leads through some vineyards and chestnut groves back to Montánchez village.

Additional remarks Apart from the described blue route and the tiny red one, there is another way-marked route: the green route. This one departs from the main roundabout at the entrance of the village and leads through a Pyrenean oak forest on the northern side of the village. The tourist office on the main plaza (plaza España) has a map of this route.

Olive groves on the slopes of the Montánchez Mountains.

Route 12: The vast steppes of La Serena

6 HOURS

Superb empty wasteland and steppe scenery.
Arid grassland birdlife that is probably unequalled by any
area in Europe.

Habitats on this route: creeks, rivers and reservoirs (p. 42); steppes (p. 48).

This route leads you right through the heart of the most important grassland area in Spain. If you take the remarks on birding in the steppes to heart (page 193), you will enjoy unforgettable sights of great and little bustards, stone curlews, calandra larks, Montagu's harriers, black-bellied sandgrouse and other steppe birds.

Departure point Cabeza del Buey

Getting there Leave in the direction of Castuera and turn right onto the small road, signposted Presa del Zujar.

1 This small road cuts like a knife through the steppes and onto the dam (*presa*) of the Zújar reservoir. Arid grassland, tawny cereal fields and ploughed land alternate and each has its own specialties. This road is the best spot to watch steppe birds, so take all the time you need. In

A young great
spotted cuckoo, one
of the magnificent
birds of the steppes
of La Serena.

spring, great bustards wade through the cereal fields or group together for their courtship rituals. Little bustards turn up every now and then, as do stone curlews. Calandra larks are simply everywhere, whereas thekla larks walk around on the ground or sit on the poles at the side of the road. Black-bellied and the more rare white-bellied sandgrouse are usually seen as fly-bys and most easily discovered by their calls. Pay attention to stone piles, as they are favoured perches for hoopoes, little owls, lesser kestrels and black-eared wheatears. The occasional Montagu's harrier scouts the fields, while higher up in the

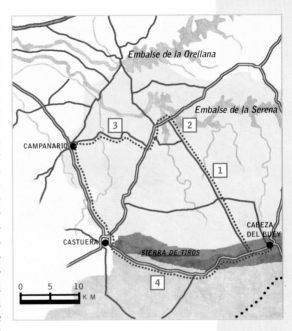

sky black kites, griffon and Egyptian vultures and the occasional golden, booted and short-toed eagle come down from the mountains in the south to hunt. Some of the big eucalyptus trees alongside the road harbour colonies of Spanish sparrows. In short, this road is an ongoing bird parade.

At about two-thirds of the way down this road, there is a drinking pool near a farm, which is frequently visited by collared pratincoles.

Close to the reservoir the road turns to the left. A smaller road goes straight ahead, towards the dam. Follow the latter.

2 You now approach the dam of the Zujar reservoir, but before you do you'll pass an abandoned house on your left hand side. Under the roof tiles several pairs of lesser kestrels and Spanish sparrows breed. The terrain surrounding the house hosts little bustards.
The road leads down to the dam and ends on the road between Castuera and the reservoir. Turn left towards Castuera. Follow this road and take the second paved road right, towards Campanario.

3 The steppes of this section of the route are entirely different from those seen before. The gently rolling hills have been replaced by steep ups and downs. Dog's teeth stand out of the ground like razor blades. This section is a little low on birds in comparison to the previous one, although raptors can appear in good numbers and black-eared wheatears use the stones as perches.

After 5 kilometres you cross a bridge over a small stream. This is a perfect place to picnic. The terrain is not fenced off and the banks of the stream are an ideal location for a stroll. Red-rumped swallows breed under the bridge and stripe-necked terrapins sunbathe on the rocks lining the stream. In winter, friar's cowl (p. 50) flowers between the dog's teeth, followed by pink foxglove* (p. 91) in May. Loose rocks shelter scolopendras and scorpions (p. 116) while Spanish marbled whites (p. 52) visit the flowers along the stream.

Further along the road you cross a stream that is sizable enough to carry a name, the Arroyo Guadalefra. It is dammed, making it a less typical place than the previous one, but a short stroll along one of the tracks can reveal similar niceties.

From here it is only five kilometres to Campanario, where you turn left towards Castuera and further towards the departure point, Cabeza del Buey.

4 The road between Castuera and Cabeza leads for the larger part along the southern slope of the Sierra de Tiros. It brings you past the village of Benquerencia, the departure point for the next route. The mountain range rises from the rolling plain to end in a rocky crest. On the rocks golden and Bonelli's eagles breed, as do a few griffon and Egyptian vultures. There is a small colony of griffons near

The collared pratincole is not a common bird in Extremadura, but can be found along the road that disects the grasslands (picture on facing page).

the village of Helechal.
But before getting there you first pass the Puerto Mejoral, which is a large gap in the mountains. During winter and early spring the Puerto is one of the best sites in la Serena, as it is the gateway through which thousands of cranes push themselves each morning to reach the dehesas in the south. The cranes spend the night on the edges of the embalses de Zujar and La Serena and feed on the acorns in the dehesas.

Additional remarks This route is easily combined with the next one. A telescope will greatly enhance your birding pleasure. Lesser kestrels breed in the town of Cabeza del Buey.

The steppes of La Serena.

Route 13: The castle and the mountains of Benquerencia

1½-2 HOURS
EASY

Amazing views over the treeless plains of La Serena. Easy encounters with birds, plants and insects typical of the lower Extremaduran mountain ranges.

Habitats on this route: the mountains (p. 62).

The castle of Benquerencia is cut out for an evening dinner in the field or a lunch as you are passing through. It is also easily combined with the previous or the next route. The scenery is simply superb and the birdlife is rich in Mediterranean rock-dwelling species.

Departure point The village of Benquerencia between Castuera and Cabeza del Buey.

The village is situated on the upper south-facing slope of the Sierra de Tiros and overlooks the dehesa-clad plains south of la Serena. Towering over it are the ruins of a castle. To visit it, follow the little signs with 'Castillo' on them.

The sombre remains of the castle are home to breeding lesser kestrels and blue rock thrushes. They hunt in the steppes of La Serena and the olive groves on the lower slopes of the mountain. Other raptors pass over every now and then, using the warm air over the south slopes. Look out for short-toed, booted, Bonelli's and golden eagles, peregrine falcons and griffon and Egyptian vultures. On clear days the views of the empty plains of La Serena are unforgettable.

A trail departs from the eastern edge of the village and leads through the olive groves on the south-facing slope. It is signposted *pinturas rupestris*, meaning 'rock paintings'. The trail is graced by mallow-leaved bindweed and colourful pasture flowers, but most interesting is the birdlife, with Orphean warblers, hoopoes and several more widespread species, such as serins and greenfinches. Crag martins wheel over your head. Check the rocks for blue rock thrushes, rock buntings and black wheatears.

A barely visible trail leads up to the rock paintings. The paintings themselves are a disappointment even with the most modest of expectations (they are practically invisible), but climbing the rocks on the right offers a view of the plains of La Serena and the mountain range to the east that is nothing less than spectacular. The difference between the north and south slope of the mountain is very visible. From here you also have the clearest view of any passing raptors. Between your feet narrow-leaved cistus and dwarf sheep's-bit flower in spring.

The south slope or *solana* (top) and the north slope or *umbría* (bottom) of the Sierra de Tiros have a profoundly different vegetation.

THE PRACTICAL PART

Route 14: La Serena, to the old mine and beyond

4 HOURS

Dry grasslands with numerous steppe birds.
Desolate ruins of a mine with a sinister colony of choughs and jackdaws.

Habitats on this route: steppes (p. 48).

This route takes you through the steppes between Castuera and Cabeza in the southern part of la Serena. It is a good second best, meaning that the route cannot compete with route 12 in terms of steppe birds and landscape. However, this route has the advantage of following a little used dirt track through areas rich in both sandgrouse, short-toed larks and rollers.

Departure point Castuera

The ruins of the old
mine of La Serena.

Getting there Follow the road towards Puebla de Alcocer, which is the main road leading through La Serena. Turn right on a good dirt track just after kilometre sign 77. It commences just after the parapet.
The track extends for about twenty kilometres and ends on the minor road between Cabeza and the Zujar reservoir, the highlight of route 12. It can be roughly divided into three different parts: the old mine, the stretch before reaching the mine and the stretch behind it.

1 Dry, sparsely vegetated steppes dominate the landscape of the first part. It is a good area to find rollers, short-toed larks, stone curlews and pin-tailed sandgrouse. The most common bird is the calandra lark, whose chattering song fills the sky in spring.

2 After ten kilometres you reach the mine, which is not much more than a pile of sand and two ruins with rock doves, kestrels, jackdaws and red-billed choughs accentuating the desolate character of the area. Bee-eaters breed in the sand pile. Some interesting plants here are rampion bellflower, sheep's-bit, a species of thrift and steppe-edelweiss.

3 Around and after the mine the percentage of cereal and ploughed fields increases. Look around for black-bellied sandgrouse, Montagu's harriers and both bustards.

Close to the other end of the dirt track, it splits. Take the branch going straight ahead over a cattle grid (the one to the right ends on private land). After 200 metres you reach another cattle grid and the track continues through the cereal fields. This last part is also good for finding great bustards.
Once back on the road, turn right and continue until you reach the main road. Turn right to head back to Castuera or left to Cabeza del Buey, with its colony of lesser kestrels occupying the town centre.

Additional remark A telescope will greatly enhance your birding pleasure.

Route 15: Touring the heart of Villuercas

6 HOURS - FULL DAY

Beautiful and quiet route through a very authentic mountain landscape.
Age-old cork and holm oak dehesas and chestnut groves.
Splendid views and birdlife near romantic castle ruins.

Habitats on this route: dehesa (p. 25); creeks, rivers and reservoirs (p. 42); the mountains (p. 62).

This scenic route is perfect for a first introduction to the Villuercas Mountains. The small mountain villages are isolated, even by Extremaduran standards. The orchards and dehesas are still used in a very traditional way. Along the way, you will pass a number of beautiful sites, with an interesting flora and a good assemblage of birds of prey.
This route offers ample possibilities to stop along the way and wander off into the mountains a little bit.

A holm oak forest in the gorge of the Portilla del Almonte. A closer look reveals that even these trees were pruned in former days.

Departure point Guadalupe

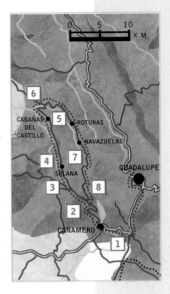

Leave Guadalupe in the direction of Cañamero.

1 The road from Guadalupe passes along a south-facing slope, covered with olive groves and stands of gum cistus. The occasional azure-winged magpie flies by to confirm the Mediterranean character of these sun-soaked slopes. However, the interesting aspects of this route are in the scenery, flora and fauna of the mid-sized mountains, which you will discover further ahead.

In Cañamero take the first right, signposted Berzacona and Navazuelas. At the next junction turn right, again signposted. Here the climb starts towards the Berzocana pass at 910 metres. The road up leads through a diverse landscape of olive, almond, fig and cherry groves, scrubland and pine and Pyrenean oak forests.

2 There are ample parking options on the deserted pass (a round-about), where you can wander into some Pyrenean oak forests, inhabited by noisy jays. Conspicuous is the lichen cover of the tree barks that flourish because of the high humidity.

Continue in the direction of Berzocana and just before reaching the village take a sharp right towards Deleitosa.

3 The stretch just before the village of *solana* leads through a beautiful, centuries-old cork oak forest with a thick undergrowth of common and Spanish white broom. Just upon reaching *solana* a track to the right leads up the mountain, from which you can explore the dehesa more quietly than from the road.

4 After *solana*, the road leads a bit away from the mountain and the cork oak dehesas are replaced by holm oaks, of an equally impressive age. Birdlife is more Mediterranean at these low altitudes, with numerous woodchat shrikes and azure-winged magpies.

Turn right towards Cabañas del Castillo.

5 Some of the nicest features of this route are the castle ruins of Cabañas del Castillo (p. 64). From Cabañas, walk towards the little village graveyard on the southern end of the village. From here, you can cross the mountain ridge and climb up to the castle from the other side. In many ways, the castle of Cabañas resembles the Castle of Monfragüe, only it is less well-known and the scenery is even more spectacular. On the rock face, dwarf sheep's-bit* and Spanish adenocarpus* grow in good numbers, while from the castle itself you have a good chance of spotting Bonelli's eagles and Peregrine falcons. Griffon vultures are not as common as in Monfragüe, but there is a small colony on the rocks a little further on.

The view from the castle is breathtaking.

Continue along the road. A little further ahead it crosses the Almonte river. Just after the bridge, turn right on the new road towards Roturas. The Almonte River is now on your right-hand side. Park in the broad shoulder of the road near the small, wooden sign 'Camino del Molino'. From here a dirt track leads down to the river.

6 The trail leads to an old mill at the base of the impressive breach of the Almonte through the mountains. This spot is reminiscent of the Peñafalcon, the breach of the Tagus through the mountains of Monfragüe. Along the trail you can find Portuguese heath, Lusitanian milkvetch, western peony, Spanish bluebell and pallid and hoop-petticoat daffodils. Check the sky for eagles, vultures and black storks.

If you didn't already lunch at the castle of Cabañas, the Almonte breach forms a good picnic spot.

Continue along the road through Roturas and onto Navazuelas.

7 If time permits, you can have a nice walk from Navazuelas into the mountains. Just after the bar 'Cuatro Caminos', a trail departs down to the Almonte creek and then up into the mountains. The valley is covered with cherry groves (which flower beautifully in April). In the chestnut groves on the mountain slope you can enjoy the flowers of western Peony, Sicilian and early purple orchids, narrow-leaved helleborine and several other plants.

Continue along the road further into the mountains. It leads up to a narrow pass at 1,061 metres before descending to the Puerto de Berzocana.

8 The higher up you go, the more the landscape becomes dominated by Spanish heath. Botanists might want to look out for small-leaved milkwort*, a beautiful purple flower, confined to the Iberian Peninsula (p. 93). It grows in clumps on the side of the road.

From Puerto de Berzacona, retrace your steps to Guadalupe.

The trunk of a Pyrenean oak. The abundance of lichens is a sign of the moist atmosphere of the Villuercas.

Route 16: The valley of the old

3 - 6 HOURS
EASY - MODERATE

One of the most unspoilt river valleys of the Villuercas.
Interesting humid river valley flora.

Habitats on this route: creeks, rivers and reservoirs (p. 42); the mountains (p. 62).

The Valle de Viejas, or valley of the old, is a hidden valley without human habitation, except for a few, hermit-like forest shags. The valley is covered with heath scrubland, Pyrenean oak forest and chestnut groves, which together make for a very attractive walk. The ecological gem is the Viejas River, on whose margins a large number of rare plants of humid habitats grow (see page 46).

The trail leading down to the Viejas River.

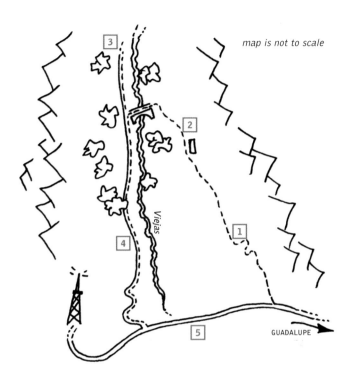

map is not to scale

Departure point Guadalupe

Getting there From Guadalupe, drive towards Navalmoral de la Mata. After a few kilometres, on top of the hill above Guadalupe, turn left towards the deserted radio station (signposted 'military base'). After 5 kilometres there is a small area where you can park. From here the trail departs to your right.

1 The trail starts in a dense scrub of Spanish heath and gum cistus with very little undergrowth. At first, the slope you descend is steep, so be wary of loose and slippery rocks. Soon the first stunted holm oaks appear. They are often completely covered with lichens and mosses, betraying a moist climate. In spring the fragile pallid narcissus* penetrates the hard soil. It will accompany you throughout the trip.

THE PRACTICAL PART

2 Further ahead you approach the Viejas River, which flows through grassy chestnut orchards and creates a splendid scenery. In the shady canopy (from May onwards) you'll find various birds of central European distribution, such as jays, nuthatches, pied flycatchers and great spotted woodpeckers. The more open and rocky spots are flowery and attract numerous butterflies. These parts are also home to the rare Schreiber's green lizard, a large animal of about 40 cm.

Along the river banks grow alders, Portuguese heath and the Portuguese laurel (see page 46). The hard-fern grows in the mossy shade.

You can cross the river on various occasions and continue along the other side until you reach a dirt track. Turning left would complete the tour within an hour. By turning right you can prolong it for another 10 kilometres (give or take). Remember that every step down means one more step up, because you will have to take the same track back.

The Viejas River

3 The Viejas Valley soon opens up and increasingly starts to show signs of habitation. Large areas of gum cistus scrubland, cherry and chestnut orchards and Pyrenean oak forests alternate. Along the open track you encounter a good number of butterflies. Red-billed choughs fly around the rocky outcrops on your left.
When turning back, stay on this track all the way until you reach the paved road to the radio station.

Sunbathing large
psammodromus.

4 The trail up is similar to the one down you started on, but the slope is much friendlier. The open track attracts some more butterflies, while Spanish bluebell, pallid narcissus* and Fernandes's narcissus* are common and conspicuous.

Upon reaching the road again, turn left for the last few metres to the departure point.

5 This last stretch is worthy of your attention too. Especially on warm spring days, the concrete gutter on your right hand side forms an ideal south-facing slope where Iberian wall lizards and large psammodromuses bask in the sun. Narrow-leaved cistus and umbel-flowered heath* border the roadside.

THE PRACTICAL PART

Route 17: Car trip through La Vera

4 HOURS - FULL DAY

Beautiful Pyrenean oak forest and sublime views over the dehesas in the plains.
Flora and fauna typical of the Extremaduran mountains.

Habitats on this route: creeks, rivers and reservoirs (p. 42); the mountains (p. 62).

This car trip offers you a good taste of the mountain landscape of La Vera, including its villages. The minor mountain roads are tranquil and offer a splendid scenery and ample possibilities for minor excursions on foot. This route stands out for its scenery, but the flora and several interesting cultural hotspots add to its attraction.

Departure point Plasencia

Getting there Leave Plasencia in the direction Avila. After 15 kilometres turn right to Casas de Castañar.

1 Near Plasencia the Mediterranean lowland dehesa atmosphere is still strongly present. But as soon as the small road winds up towards Casas de Castañar, this drastically changes. The landscape consists of cherry and almond groves, green, moist meadows, forest patches and little streams lined with narrow-leaved ash, breathing the air of a cool and fertile mountain landscape. From the little bushes rufous nightingales and melodious warblers sing. Just before Casas there are a few meadows and chestnut groves with orchids in them, including Sicilian, champagne, tongue and early purple orchids.

From Casas de Castañar, continue towards Cabrero and Piornal.

2 The landscape changes and becomes dominated by young Pyrenean oak forests and the occasional scrubland patch of Spanish heath. After Piornal you reach the mountain ridge and start descending down the other side. This part is covered by a beautiful Pyrenean oak forest, interspersed with little creeks. Here and there massive, old chestnuts are scattered in the forest. All of them are pruned, indicating that this land was intensively used in former times. The forest floor has an interesting flora in spring.

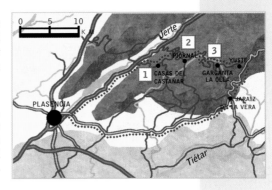

3 Continuing down the road, you reach the picturesque mountain village of Garganta la Olla. From here, there are several hiking possibilities into the mountains of La Vera.

Once in Garganta, turn left and immediately left again to follow the minor road towards the Yuste Monastery, where the emperor Carlos V spent his final days. The road towards the monastry leads through another Pyrenean oak forest, but being located at a lower altitude and facing the south, the seasonal cycle has advanced much further. The beautiful monastery is worth a visit.

Continuing along the road from Yuste, you will soon reach the end at the larger road, connecting Plasencia with Jarandilla de la Vera. Turn left and follow the road back to Plasencia.

Additional remarks If time permits, you could prolong this trip by taking the beautiful minor road to Bazagona and visit Monfragüe (Portilla de Tiétar: route 1, point 6).

From each of the villages along this route, hiking trails depart into the mountains. If you wish to explore more of La Vera on foot, these are good departure points.

The creek near Garganta la Olla.

Route 18: Garganta de los Infiernos

6 HOURS
MODERATE

Alpine landscape with groves, forests, mountain scrubland
and an idyllic river gorge.
A rich flora and butterfly fauna.

Habitats on this route: creeks, rivers and reservoirs (p. 42); the mountains (p. 62).

Walking in the mountains and in the deeply cut river valleys of the Garganta de los Infiernos nature reserve is most interesting between mid-April and late November. You will be treated to an alpine landscape that is so unlike the sun-baked dehesas and steppe land of the valley that it is hard to believe that they are only 50 kilometres apart.

Of several possible routes (see additional remarks) we describe the most scenic and classic one. There is a map of all the way-marked routes freely available at the tourist booth at the northern end of the village of Jerte. This route largely corresponds with the blue route on this map.

Red-flowered
spurge*, a typical
and abundant flower
of the higher slopes
of the Garganta de
los Infiernos.

Departure point Jerte village

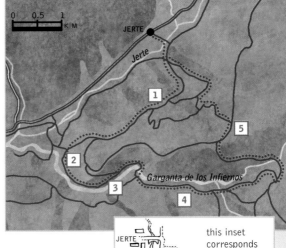

Walk through the old village towards the river and cross it via the only bridge in the village centre (birdwatchers might want to linger in search of grey wagtails and dippers). After the bridge, turn right and follow the track lining the cherry and chestnut groves. There are a few tracks you ought to ignore (see inset of the map).

1 During the first section of this beautiful walk you remain in the valley of the Jerte. On your right-hand side are some of the famous Valle de Jerte cherry groves that flower in early April. To the left the hillside is covered with chestnut groves. In May the forest soil is covered by a beautiful carpet of wildflowers, such as Spanish bluebell, white flax, Solomon's seal and numerous purple and Sicilian orchids. Narrow-leaved helleborine (an orchid with pure-white, nearly closed flowers) is also common. On moist spring mornings, keep an eye open for fire salamanders rummaging through the leaf litter.

The trail ends on a small, paved forest track. Follow it to the left.

2 The track winds around the mountain and into the valley of the Garganta de los Infiernos, a side valley of the Jerte valley. The trail follows the south-facing slope. Open patches, overgrown with scrubland of Spanish heath and French lavender, are interesting for butterfly enthusiasts. Wall lizards and large psammodromuses sunbathe on the trail. Pyrenean oak forests dominate the forested patches. A thick layer of bracken fern, under which very few other plants grow, covers the ground. Only the bright blue shrubby gromwell (p. 19) is conspicuous.

A trail splits off to the right towards the river. Follow it.

3 Alder trees and willow thickets occupy the banks of the quick-flowing river, from which rufous nightingales and melodious warblers sing. The trail follows the riverside to a high bridge over the stream. There are several natural pools in the river here, in which the villagers bathe in summer. When there are no visitors, keep an eye on the rocks in the river. With some luck you can spot grey wagtails, a dipper or a beautifully coloured Schreiber's green lizard; with even more luck an otter. The stream is also home to the Pyrenean desman (see mammal section on page 101), but its nocturnal habits make it very difficult to find.

Across the bridge, the trail winds up the mountain on the other, north-facing slope. During the next section you gain altitude rapidly.

The Garganta de los Infiernos supports a rich butterfly fauna. This burnets companion, actually a day-active moth, is one of the many species.

4 Rocks, pasture and a few bushes of Pyrenean oak cover the slope you are on right now. The pasture is grazed by sheep and, in winter, most likely by ibex coming down from higher altitudes. Red-flowered spurge* is a conspicuous plant in spring. For botanists it is worth exploring the rocky fields and cliffs for the rare Gredos' snapdragon* and Spanish adenocarpus, and the moist pastures for Gredos gentian*. On sunny spots, keep an eye open for butterflies, including the rare yellow-banded skipper. Birds are represented by melodious, Sardinian, Dartford and subalpine warblers, rock buntings, rock thrushes and blue rock thrushes. Don't forget to look up in the air. Golden eagles and honey buzzards breed nearby and of course griffon vultures can appear as well.

Further on, the trail crosses another stream, coming from a side valley. Cross the stream (this is a good spot for Schreiber's green lizards) and follow the Garganta de los Infiernos valley towards Puente Nuevo. Cross this picturesque bridge (again the river is worth exploring for dippers, grey wagtails and Schreiber's green lizards) and follow the trail, which now again follows the south-facing slope.

5 The last long stretch brings you back through Pyrenean oak forest and some open scrubland patches to the Jerte village. The trail first gains a little more altitude, until you are on the mountain that flanks Jerte village. The last stretch offers a similar flora and fauna as the way up.

Take the third track left, leading down into the valley and back to Jerte village.

Additional remarks In summer, weekends and during holidays an increasingly large group of Spanish tourists flee their hot cities for the mountains. Animals either retreat higher into the mountains or limit their activities to the early or late hours. Especially in summer, the high mountains become much more interesting than the forested valleys.

Other tour options There are several other nice routes departing from Jerte, descriptions of which are available at the tourist office. A true high-altitude hike departs from Tornavacas at the border between Extremadura and Castilla - León. A description of this route is also available at the tourist office in Jerte.

Pyrenean oak forest (left) and the creek of the Garganta de los Infiernos (right) are two habitats that characterise this route.

THE PRACTICAL PART

Interesting sites and other extras

Extra route in Monfragüe Apart from the described routes there is an other trail departing from Villarreal de San Carlos. It runs between the minor road towards Saltos de Torrejón and the Tiétar River and ends at the Tejadilla observation hut, next to the dam over the Tiétar. The trail is sandwiched between the road and the reservoir and is not nearly as nice as the other three trails. But this doesn't mean that it is uninteresting. The trail (indicated with yellow markings) leads through some nice, shrubby holm oak dehesas and passes several shady creeks along the way.

Almonte River A classic spot for a little stroll is at the bridge over the Almonte River halfway between Torrejón el Rubio and Trujillo. You can walk about one hundred metres in both directions along the river, passing through some exceptionally nice and flowery holm oak dehesas. The Almonte river is a good spot to observe bee-eaters, cirl buntings, hoopoes, black storks, most raptors, most amphibians, stripe-necked terrapins, viperine snakes and more. It also makes a scenic picnic spot.

A visit to the old town centre of Trujillo with its many storks is highly recommended.

Trujillo Trujillo is a small, romantic town on a granite hill in the middle of some of the finest steppes of Extremadura. It is the hometown of Pizarro, one of the famous conquistadores, and has a beautiful town centre and a huge, partly renovated castle with a splendid view over the steppes. Lesser kestrels, pallid swifts and white storks breed in large numbers.

Cáceres Cáceres is the capital of the similarly named northern province of Extremadura. It is a university city with a lively urban culture and a beautiful and intact walled medieval centre, which gives the town its status as a UNESCO site. White storks and lesser kestrels breed in the old centre.

Guadalupe The lovely mountain village of Guadalupe is dominated by a huge monastery surrounded by small, medieval streets. The monastery is famous as a place of worship and holds some cultural treasures. Its roofs are home to a sizable colony of lesser kestrels.

Other tour options in Sierra de las Villuercas There are more tracks and valleys to explore than the two described in this guidebook. From Guadalupe you can walk along the minor entrance road and turn onto a track that leaves to the right at the (only) hairpin curve. The track leads along a shady river and forms a lovely evening stroll.
Other beautiful explorations can be found further afield. Northeast of Guadalupe lies a beautiful valley and mountain range, called the Sierra del Obispo. A minor road leads off the Guadalupe - Castañar de Ibor road and up to the Obispo pass.
At the southern edge of Castañar de Ibor, in a curve, a track leaves towards the east. This is a good place to find some of the orchids of las Villuercas.

Mérida Mérida is the ancient capital of the Roman province of Lusitania. Here you can find the most intact amphitheatre in all of Spain, as well as some other Roman structures. Mérida is also the capital of Extremadura and a lively city. The town has also something to offer on the nature front. Alpine swifts breed in the Roman bridge over the Guadiana River. This bridge overlooks an islet in the river with a mixed colony of cattle egrets and night herons.

Sites further afield

Sierra de Gata and Las Hurdes The western part of Extremadura's northern border is formed by a large mountain range, known as Sierra de Gata and Las Hurdes. This remote and heavily forested region is home to a relict population of Iberian lynx and maybe even wolves, as well as harbouring numerous interesting plants, including some endemics. There are also fair numbers of birds of prey in the Sierra de Gata, including black vultures and golden, Bonelli's and Spanish imperial eagles.

Llanos de Brozas Next to the Llanos de Cáceres and La Serena, the Llanos de Brozas forms the third large expanse of arid grassland in Extremadura. Hundreds of great bustards, around one thousand little bustards, several hundreds of pin-tailed and black-bellied sandgrouse and numerous Montagu's harriers occupy the steppes and dry cereal cultivations. In winter, several thousands of cranes reside in the plains. The minor roads between Brozas and Herreruela and between Brozas and Aliseda yield the best chance of success.

Sierra de San Pedro Some of the finest cork and holm oak dehesas are found in the Sierra de San Pedro, between Cáceres and Mérida. The Sierra de San Pedro has one of the highest numbers of breeding pairs of Spanish imperial eagles and black vultures. Orchids are also well-represented. Nice roads run between Aliseda and Alburquerque and between Aliseda and the Cáceres - Badajóz road.

Cornalvo Just northeast of Mérida lies the embalse de Cornalvo, a small reservoir with a Roman dam amidst a typical holm oak dehesa. The reservoir with surrounding landscape is a nature reserve. There is a trail around the reservoir.

Sierra Grande de Hornachos The small mountain range near the village of Hornachos, some 50 kilometres southeast of Mérida, is another Monfragüe-like area. Hornachos also exhibits a strong difference between *umbría* (north-slope) and *solana* (south-slope) vegetation. The south slope is very bare and rocky, perfect for reptiles and rock-dwelling birds. A way-marked trail leads through the finer part of the reserve and departs from Hornachos village.

The often centuries-old stonewalls are both a living monument of the past and a refuge for a number of birds and reptiles.

Tourist information & observation tips

When to go

The best period for a visit to Extremadura is between April and mid-June. In April most wildflowers are in bloom and May is the birds' prime breeding season.

Between November and February the cranes and other northern guests are present, making winter an attractive period as well. In February and March it is early spring, which is another interesting time. The first summer visitors, such as swallows, short-toed eagles and black storks, are arriving while the cranes are moving out. Hoop-petti-coat daffodils are flowering everywhere and the first orchids appear. March is also the best time to find great spotted cuckoos, which become elusive in May.

Visiting Extremadura in summer

Unfortunately for all those tied to the summer months for their holiday, July and August are the least suitable months for a visit to Extremadura.

In summer, Mediterranean nature is temporarily under the spell of the dry, tropical winds. Rain, even the smallest drop, is rare. Temperatures easily rise well above 40°C, all annual plants have been scorched away and the plains look like a true African savannah.

However, this does not mean that there is nothing to see. Summer is the perfect time to find reptiles and insects. The elusive sandgrouse is also most easily spotted in the summer months, when they visit pools and reservoirs at set times (try the Embalse de Talaván and Embalse de Guadiloba on route 8 at dusk or dawn). The other summer birds are visible as well, although they are not as active as in spring and are therefore a little harder to spot.

When visiting Extremadura in summer, you do best to go out in the early morning and late evening. The afternoons yield nothing more than heat haze and heat stroke. Furthermore, within the summer early July is the better month for nature, because the flowering and breeding season in the mountains hasn't ended yet. The upper regions in the Sierra de Gredos and Garganta are at their peak in June.

Where to stay

Extremadura has a wealth of rural lodges in the most remote and picturesque villages, a situation strongly promoted by the Extremaduran government. A list of these facilities is readily available in the back of this book.

Unfortunately, if you enjoy camping the options are much more limited. There is a good and popular campsite north of Monfragüe, along the Trujillo - Plasencia road near Malpartida de Plasencia. A list of campsites is also available at the back of this book.

Visitors' centres

There are visitors' centres in the town centres of all major cities in Extremadura. In addition, you'll find small visitors' centres in Villarreal and Torrejón (for Monfragüe), Guadalupe (for Sierra de las Villluercas), Jaraiz and Jarandilla (for La Vera), Jerte (for Valle de Jerte and Garganta de los Infiernos) and Cabeza del Buey and Castuera (for La Serena)

Getting around

The car is the most comfortable means of transport in Extremadura. Distances are long, temperatures are high and towns are far apart. Steppe birds are least shy when approached by car, because they cannot see your movements and therefore do not see you as a threat. At the departure points of the hiking routes, parking is rarely a problem. In other words, Extremadura seems to be designed for cars.

However, if you are experienced and have an adventurous outlook on life, the bike is an attractive alternative. The advantage of the bike is that at a pace of 15 to 20 kilometres an hour, you miss very little of the wildlife along the way. Natural treasures can be enjoyed from anywhere along the road.

If you decide to try your luck with public transportation, bring a good book, because you will inevitably be spending quite some time in dull bus stops. Unfortunately for anyone travelling on a low budget, the public transport system is poorly developed. It is not hard to get to Trujillo, Cáceres or the Monfragüe train station (the latter is near Malpartida de Plasencia, 15 kilometres from the Monfragüe nature park), but options to get to the nature park or Torrejón are limited. Most villages can be reached by bus, but departures are often only once or twice a week and at odd times. If you do decide to give it a try, you would do well to learn some Spanish and to ask around in the local pubs, since the information from the villagers is more reliable than the scarce schedules.

Hitchhiking is another option. In our experience, getting rides is usually not too hard, although guarantees obviously cannot be given. If you speak some Spanish and do not look too much like a tourist, your chances will improve, especially outside the spring tourist season. Remember that hitchhiking always carries a risk. The Extremaduran people are usually friendly, but one has to remain careful, especially single female travellers.

Maps

The best map of Extremadura is the 1:400,000 Michelin map of central Spain, which will be sufficient for planning your overall trip and for getting you from one region to the next.

For the proposed routes, the maps in this book suffice, but in addition there are local maps, usually free, available at local information centres. They show alternative routes in the region and can be an interesting addition.

Permits and entrance fees

There are no reserves requiring a permit or an entrance fee.

Annoyances and hazards

The chances of stumbling upon a poisonous animal in Extremadura are very small, unless you are actively looking for them. A scorpion's sting or a scolopendra bite is painful but not dangerous. The same goes for the bite of the Lataste's viper, the only poisonous snake in Extremadura. Be aware, however, that non-poisonous snake bites are also painful and are quite often followed by infections.

When going out on hikes, be wary of heat stroke and sunburns. These are the most common ways of ending a day uncomfortably. Take measures in the form of sufficient sun block. You should also consider bringing a hat or sun cap along with you on your trip. Bringing enough water (1½ litres pp/pd at the very least) and enough salty and energy-rich food are other musts. During bad weather, stones can become slippery when wet. Loose gravel is the rule rather than the exception, so it is recommended that you wear good and high boots that support your ankles.

Another thing to be aware of is the traffic. The new, smooth roads with only few curves encourage speeding and discourage birdwatching. Be careful not to let your enthusiasm for birdwatching lead you to pulling over on potentially dangerous spots.

Plant-hunting regions

The visitor who has come to Extremadura to find rare and interesting plants will want to focus on the mountains rather than on the lowlands. The Sierra de las Villuercas (routes 15 and 16) and La Vera (17 and 18) are most interesting.

To be more precise, the Valle de Viejas (route 16) is the best place in the Villuercas for the plants of cool, damp river valleys, such as the Portuguese laurel. The region around Berzacona and Cabañas del Castillo (route 15) is another hotspot, with enclaves of central European plants like bastard balm, round-leaved sundew and the beautiful Iberian endemics Spanish lupin and small-leaved milkwort*. Then there is the Valle del Obispo and the chestnut groves in the valley on the southern edge of Castañar de Ibor. In the latter, you will find hundreds of orchids and will also enjoy a beautiful walk. In La Vera, the Garganta de los Infiernos (route 18) is very attractive, since it offers all sorts of middle and high altitude species, including Gredos' snapdragon*, Gredos gentian*, Heywood's foxglove* and red-flowered spurge*.

Monfragüe has a smashing flora as well. Especially the north-slope (Umbría) vegetations are botanical jewels with, in addition to a diverse shrub and tree vegetation, beautiful herbs like green-flowered birthwort*, Spanish fritillary, wild tulip, and Lang's and dense-flowered orchids. Routes 2, 3 and 4, also in Monfragüe, make good botanical excursions too.

The town of Zafra in southern Extremadura is surrounded by a limestone region with some unique plants. For those who do not wish to travel that far, the region around Almaráz (route 1) and the region known as 'La Alberca' also have a lot to offer. The latter region is in fact a large hill, which is located east of Cáceres and west of the village of Sierra de Fuentes. Some interesting plants here are red toad-flax, Spanish iris and numerous orchids, including woodcock, mirror, yellow and bee orchids. The large region of the Sierra de San Pedro is interesting to explore as well, if you are interested in orchids.

Another very good plant-hunting region is the Sierra Fría near Valencia de Alcántara (right next to the Portuguese border, west from Cáceres). This 'Atlantic island in the Mediterranean', as it is popularly called among botanists, hosts a number of rare plants of a typical southern Atlantic distribution, including the odd Portuguese sundew, Kerry lily and Portuguese viper's bugloss*.

Finding snakes, spiders, scorpions and the like

For the uninitiated, this is how you do it.

Find yourself a stony field or dehesa and start turning over the stones. Underneath them you find a wonderful hidden life of creatures that appear on too many menus to be able to afford themselves a place under the sun. Thus they take refuge under a rock, only coming out at night to hunt.

You will mostly encounter ants and their nests, but every now and then you will find scorpions, tarantulas, snakes, scolopendras and scutigeras*. If you are lucky you might even stumble upon a worm lizard, a snake in hiding or one of the more drought-resistant amphibians.

Turning over flat stones of over 20 by 20 centimetres yields the most success. Lift them up on one side, turn them over and step back. Be aware that some animals can sting or bite painfully (see annoyances and hazards). Never hold the overtur-ned stone in your hand, because the animal might be underneath it and crawl up your sleeve.

Turning over stones is rather like unwrapping Christmas gifts: it is exciting, high-ly addictive and there is always one more ahead that must hide something good. Be aware that turning over stones is also very invasive for the animals that are hiding. Many of them worked hard to create a little nest underground. Therefore, make sure that you don't disturb the subterranean life too long and place the stone back in exactly the same position as you found it.

Some snakes are active at night (see reptiles and amphibians section on page 116). These often warm themselves on the pavement of small country roads. A drive or walk at dusk can reveal ladder, false and southern smooth snakes. In spring other snakes and lizards use these places to warm up for the day.

Finding amphibians

The amphibians in Extremadura lead a rather hidden life, but if you are in the right place at the right time, they appear by the hundreds. Small roads and tracks near rivers are the right places; moist evenings in autumn, winter and, to a lesser extent, spring are the right times. These are the periods when toads and newts travel to their mating pools and cross the streets by the hundreds.

The more drought-resistant species hide under stones at the bottom of pools that are drying out. Carefully check the flat stones at the edges that are still moist. Here you might find sharp-ribbed salamanders, Southern marbled newts, western spadefoots and Iberian midwife toads. Be extra careful in placing back the stones, as a toad or newt is easily squashed.

Birdwatching in the steppes

If you have no experience birdwatching in the steppes, here are some suggestions. First of all, go out early in the morning or late in the evening, when the sun is just coming up or almost going down. At these times of day, the light (and thereby the scenery) is most beautiful, the birds are most active and the air is not shimmering with heat haze.

The best way to find birds is to drive slowly along the small steppe roads. In spring, roll down your windows to hear the bird sounds (this is the way to find little bustards and sandgrouse). Stop at good vantage points (hill tops, etc.) and scan the area with your binoculars to find birds on the ground. A telescope makes birdwatching in the steppes much more interesting.

Birds are easily chased away by movements. It is best not to leave your car, but if you do, stay low and next to the car to prevent the birds from detecting your movements.

If you want to explore the steppes on foot, you do best to choose a place with a creek and some dog's teeth. Here you have the best opportunity to see insects, reptiles and plants and run the least risk of disturbing vulnerable steppe species such as great bustards.

Responsible tourism

'Take nothing but your photo, leave nothing but your footprint', is the well-known phrase that summarizes the idea of responsible tourism. It goes without saying that, as a visitor to a nature reserve, you have a responsibility to leave your surroundings and everything in it undisturbed. But maybe it is less obvious what is and isn't hazardous in the case of Extremadura. So here is what you should be especially aware of when visiting this area.

The nature of Extremadura is strongly connected to the traditional land use, as you can read in the dehesa and history sections. To help maintain these ecosystems, you can use the products coming from it, so that their production remains ecologically viable. Eat local food, drink local wine and stay in rural hostels (casas rurales; see list on page 200) or small hotels or camp sites.

TOURIST INFORMATION & OBSERVATION TIPS

When going out into the fields, it is important to respect private property. For many local landowners nature tourists and nature conservationists are one and the same, so often you will be regarded as an ambassador of nature conservation. If you do not respect the private property rights of landowners, this reflects negatively on nature conservation. Since most ecologically valuable areas are on private property, the owner's attitude is of vital importance for nature conservation.

Some shy bird species are under pressure, most notably bustards and several eagles. When making a trip in the steppes, keep a low profile. If you encounter great or little bustards near the road, do not leave your car, because you will chase them away. Other vulnerable birds breed on ledges in rock faces. Be careful when approaching rocky slopes that you do not disturb the nests of breeding birds.

Nearby destinations worth a visit

Outside Extremadura the most interesting nature destinations are either to the north or to the south. When southbound, you cross the Andalusian border and beyond the dehesa-clad Sierra Morena you enter the coastal plain of the Guadalquivir river. On the Atlantic coast lie the extensive salt marshes of the Coto Doñana. This bird hotspot offers a completely different nature and atmosphere than Extremadura, with wide-open mudflats and dusty, sun-baked umbrella pine forests. The best spots to visit are described in the Crossbill Guide to the Coto Doñana.

Just east of the Coto Doñana, there is a series of beautiful natural areas in the mountains known as 'Serranía de Ronda'. These mountains on the Mediterranean coast are renowned for their scenic beauty, unique flora (including many orchids) and vivid culture. The Serranía de Ronda is extensively described in the Crossbill Guide to the Andalusian Sierras.

A very different landscape awaits the traveller going north. First of all, there is the Sierra de Gredos reserve, which can be reached by driving through the Jerte valley and then turning east at the town of El Barco. The reserve can be entered from the village of Hoyos del Espino. The Sierra de Gredos is a high altitude reserve with of number of trails through which you can enjoy its wild landscape, flora and fauna. Being such an isolated mountain region, the Sierra de Gredos has a number of unique plants and animals, including the Iberian ibex.

Further up north you travel through the huge upland plain of Castilla la Mancha, where you can see even more great bustards than in Extremadura. The area near the town of Villafáfila is the best spot. From here, the Picos de Europa are not far away anymore. For a naturalist it would be interesting to compare the Picos de Europa -a high altitude mountain range with a distinct central European character- with the Mediterranean mountains of the Sierra de Gredos. Travelling east from here you reach the Pyrenees and the dry plains of the River Ebro, two other gems of European nature.

Typical dehesa dishes

Usually dinner tips are beyond the scope of our guidebooks, but for Extremadura we make an exception. The reason is that the valuable dehesa ecosystem is firmly tied to the farming products derived from it. Dehesas can only survive with the production of these items and, in turn, they need people to order them. Here are a few dishes that are very typical, very tasty and very environmentally sound.

Jamón ibérico de bellota The famous air-dried ham of Extremadura. A world-famous species of ham, but very expensive. The *de bellota* part means acorn-fed. Less expensive and still very good is *Jamón ibérico*, which means that the pig is of the typical Spanish black pig race. *Jamón serrano* is cheaper still, but the origin of the meat is often unclear and the quality can thus vary considerably. *Jamón* is nice on bread but is also used in several dishes.

Revuelto con Jamón ibérico y espárragos silvestres Scrambled eggs with ham and wild asparagus. A tasty mixture, usually generously supplied with the wild (green) asparagus and ham in comparison to the egg. The variety with mushrooms (*setas*) is a delicacy as well, just like *Revuelto de cardillas*, which is prepared with the basal leaves of the golden thistle.

Caldereta de cordero or cabrito Lamb (*cordero*) or young goat (*cabrito*) stew. A tasty stew of meat and usually potatoes, served with bread.

Criadillas A kind of wild truffle, collected in the dehesas. A delicious ingredient in many dishes.

Queso de cabra and Queso de oveja Goat cheese and sheep cheese respectively. There are many different delicious locally-made goat and sheep cheeses, so you can try a new variety in every village you visit.

Queso fresco con membrillo Cottage cheese with a kind of pear marmalade. A dessert.

Torta A soft, mild Camembert-like sheep cheese. Just like the other cheeses it is locally-made and often sold as *Torta del Casar*; cheese of the house.

Liquor de bellota Very sweet liquor made of acorns (*bellota* in Spanish). It is very typical for Extremadura, but hardly authentic, because the *liquor de bellota* is a rather new invention, primarily distilled for the tourist market.

Birdwatching list

The numbers between the brackets () refer to the routes on page 128 onwards:

Herons and egrets Little egrets are present every now and then along streams and reservoirs. Cattle egrets are mostly found in the steppes (around Trujillo, 8) and La Serena (12). Cattle egrets and night herons breed on an island in the centre of Mérida.

Ducks and grebes Smaller reservoirs such as the Embalse de Talaván and marshes near Almaráz (1).

White and black storks The white stork breeds in varying numbers in almost all the villages. Famous breeding spots are the town centres of Cáceres and Trujillo (8), Los Barruecos (9) and the umbrella pines near Monroy (5). The Black stork breeds in Monfragüe on the Peñafalcon (1, 2), where it is most easily found, and also throughout the mountains and older dehesas of Extremadura. In September they congregate in large numbers on the edges of reservoirs, such as the Embalse de Guadiloba (8) and La Serena (12).

Vultures The Griffon vulture can be spotted everywhere, even from a terrace on the plaza mayor in Trujillo. The Black vulture is a common breeder in Monfragüe (1, 2, 3, 4), but is often more numerous in the steppes where it feeds (8, 10). The Egyptian vulture is less common, although far from rare. They, and (?) are concentrated in and around Monfragüe (1, 3, 5, 7, 8) and sometimes breed on Peñafalcon (1, 2) and Portilla del Tietar (1).

Eagles Booted and short-toed eagles are typical dehesa birds and the most numerous of the eagles. They can be observed on routes 1, 5, 6, 7, 8, 9, 10, 12, 14. The golden eagle is a less common mountain bird (1, 13, 15, 16, 17, 18). The Spanish Imperial eagle is a tricky one to spot. Monfragüe and surrounding dehesas offer the best opportunities to observe this bird. It often breeds on or near the electricity towers west of Torrejón el Rubio. In 2005 it also nested on Portilla del Tiétar (1). Finally, Bonelli's eagle is also a rare mountain bird. Villarreal and Cerro Gimio in Monfragüe (1, 3) and route 13 are usually good for spotting this bird; Cabañas del Castillo (15) is the best.

Montagu's harrier Rather common in steppes (8, 10, 12, 14).

Kites Red kites are common in winter and rather rare in spring and summer. The black kite is the most numerous bird of prey from March onwards. The black-shouldered kite is a highly unpredictable bird in that it is common in some years in some spots and absent in others. In general it prefers cereal fields in open dehesas and other small-scale agricultural land. It's best to ask other bird-watchers about its whereabouts. The classic sites are near Monroy and especially the olive groves of Talaván (5).

Lesser kestrel and merlin The lesser kestrel is common in the steppes (8, 12). It has sizable colonies in the town centres of Trujillo and Cáceres. It also breeds in the castle of Benquerencia (13). Merlins winter in small but steady numbers in the steppes.

Peregrine falcon The peregrine falcon is a frequent but uncommon breeder in all Extremaduran mountain ranges. You can find it in Monfragüe (1, 2, 3) and Benquerencia (13), but most reliably in Cabañas del Castillo (15).

Purple gallinule Uncommon but increasing in Almaráz (1).

Common Crane From November to early March, cranes feed in small family groups in dehesas (common between Torrejón and Monroy and to Jaraicejo). Their morning and evening migrations to and from the night roosts can be very well observed at the Embalse de Talaván and the Puerto de Mejoral (12, 14).

Bustards In spring the great bustard is an almost certain bet on routes 10 and 12, provided you are a bit experienced in birdwatching in the steppes. Route 7 and 14 are also good places. The little bustard is more common and occurs, in addition to the above-mentioned routes, in Los Barruecos (8). In winter, bustards form large groups and behave less conspicuously, making them harder to find. On the other hand, wintertime sometimes yields a group of feeding bustards right next to the car...

Stone curlew Common but hard-to-spot birds that breed in grassy steppes and open dehesas (7, 8, 9, 10, 12, 14)

Waders, gulls and terns Extremadura is not the best of places for these birds. Common sandpiper and little ringed plover frequent the borders of streams and black-winged stilts the reservoir shores. Dotterel sometimes winters in or passes through the steppes (8, 10, 12). The little tern breeds in the Embalse de Guadiloba.

Sandgrouse Most common in La Serena (12, 14). The black-bellied sandgrouse prefers recently ploughed fields. The pin-tailed sandgrouse occurs in scanty (not grassy) steppes. However, it is when they are flying that sandgrouse are usually seen, drawing your attention by their conspicuous and resounding flight-calls. Especially in summer it becomes easier to spot them, as they fly to their drinking pools in early morning and late evening. The Embalse de Talaván and Embalse de Guadiloba (8) are the spots to go to.

Lesser kestrel and merlin The lesser kestrel is common in the steppes (8, 12). It has sizable colonies in the town centres of Trujillo and Cáceres. It also breeds in the castle of Benquerencia (13). Merlins winter in small but steady numbers in the steppes.

Peregrine falcon The peregrine falcon is a frequent but uncommon breeder in all Extremaduran mountain ranges. You can find it in Monfragüe (1, 2, 3) and Benquerencia (13), but most reliably in Cabañas del Castillo (15).

Purple gallinule Uncommon but increasing in Almaráz (1).

Common Crane From November to early March, cranes feed in small family groups in dehesas (common between Torrejón and Monroy and to Jaraicejo). Their morning and evening migrations to and from the night roosts can be very well observed at the Embalse de Talaván and the Puerto de Mejoral (12, 14).

Bustards In spring the great bustard is an almost certain bet on routes 10 and 12, provided you are a bit experienced in birdwatching in the steppes. Route 7 and 14 are also good places. The little bustard is more common and occurs, in addition to the above-mentioned routes, in Los Barruecos (8). In winter, bustards form large groups and behave less conspicuously, making them harder to find. On the other hand, wintertime sometimes yields a group of feeding bustards right next to the car...

Stone curlew Common but hard-to-spot birds that breed in grassy steppes and open dehesas (7, 8, 9, 10, 12, 14)

Waders, gulls and terns Extremadura is not the best of places for these birds. Common sandpiper and little ringed plover frequent the borders of streams and black-winged stilts the reservoir shores. Dotterel sometimes winters in or passes through the steppes (8, 10, 12). The little tern breeds in the Embalse de Guadiloba.

Sandgrouse Most common in La Serena (12, 14). The black-bellied sandgrouse prefers recently ploughed fields. The pin-tailed sandgrouse occurs in scanty (not grassy) steppes. However, it is when they are flying that sandgrouse are usually seen, drawing your attention by their conspicuous and resounding flight-calls. Especially in summer it becomes easier to spot them, as they fly to their drinking pools in early morning and late evening. The Embalse de Talaván and Embalse de Guadiloba (8) are the spots to go to.

Great spotted cuckoo Best seen between February and April in areas with lots of common magpies, especially around the granite boulders near Trujillo and Cáceres (8, 9 and 10) and in La Serena (12 and 14).

Owls The little owl is very common in the steppes and the areas with granite boulders (8, 9, 10, 12 and 14), sitting on stone walls, rocks and posts. The barn owl commonly breeds in villages and shags. Scops owl is hard to spot, but the soft 'Pjuup' call is often heard after sunset. The eagle owl commonly breeds in rock cliffs in mountains and river valleys. The Portilla de Tiétar is a classic locality. Ask other birdwatchers for the recent location of the nest.

Red-necked nightjar Common in the dehesas. A good spot is the Embalse de Torrejón (7) at dusk. The call is an unmistakable, far-carrying ka-TOK ka-TOK.

Swifts The Alpine swift is not uncommon. Classic localities are in Monfragüe (near the bridge over the Tagus and on routes 1 and 2; best chance when early) and the Roman bridge in Mérida and Cabañas del Castillo (route 14). Pallid swifts are, just like common swifts, numerous in the town centres, notably in Trujillo. The white-rumped swift is occasionally seen near the Castle of Monfragüe (2), but arrives late in the year.

Bee-eater, roller and hoopoe Hoopoes and bee-eaters are very common in the dehesas. The roller is mostly a steppe bird, but has become rather rare. It is still fairly numerous in La Serena (10, 12) and north of Cáceres, on the road towards Torrejón.

Larks The skylark is a common winter visitor; wood larks and crested larks are numerous breeders in the dehesas. The Thekla lark breeds mostly in the steppes, but also in dehesas. Calandra larks are common in the steppes. Last in line is the short-toed lark. It is rather rare and occurs in very scanty, wasteland-like steppes in La Serena (12).

Blue rock thrush Common on rocky mountain slopes, such as in Monfragüe (1, 2 ,3, 4) and Sierra de Tiros (13) and Villuercas (15).

Black and black-eared wheatears The black-eared wheatear is the most numerous wheatear. It breeds in steppes with lots of rocks. The black wheatear is restricted to dry, rocky slopes and ruins. The crests of low mountains, such as Monfragüe (2) and Sierra de Tiros (13) are good spots. Rocky river valleys, such as the one near Monroy, are other favoured areas.

'Brown' warblers Zitting cisticolas and Cetti's warblers are confined to damp areas. Zitting cisticolas are most numerous in meadows, while Cetti's warblers retreat in thickets, preferably with bramble, along rivers. Melodious warblers are typical in trees and olive groves of the lower mountains (11 and 13). Olivaceous warblers are rare, but occur essentially in the same terrain.

Sylvia warblers Sardinian and Dartford warblers are common scrubland birds. The Sardinian occurs in nearly any kind of scrubland; the Dartford mostly in low scrubland with single trees. Subalpine warblers are most common in mountain scrubland. The Orphean warbler is an uncommon bird proper to trees and olive groves in the lower mountains (11 and 13).

Shrikes Woodchat shrikes are common in dehesas; southern grey shrikes are less numerous and more drawn to open terrain.

Azure-winged magpie, red-billed chough and raven The azure-winged magpie is everywhere in the dehesas. Ravens and red-billed choughs occur on rocky mountain slopes, for example the Castillo of Monfragüe (2). Choughs are also numerous in the old mine of La Serena (14).

Spanish and rock sparrows The rock sparrow is fairly rare and most likely to be found in dry river beds in dehesas and steppes, for example in the dehesas just south of Monfragüe. The Spanish sparrow is common locally, for example in the large Eucalyptus trees in La Serena (route 12) and in the umbrella pines near Monroy (5).

Buntings The corn bunting is excessively common in any lowland. Rock buntings are fairly common on rocky slopes (1, 2, 3, 4, 13, 15, 16, 18). The Cirl bunting is rather uncommon in the dehesas, often on slopes near water (for example on the Almonte river, near the bridge of the Trujillo-Torrejón road).

Casas rurales / Rural lodging

Abadia	las eras	927484085
Acebo	las martas	927141685
info@lasmartas.com		
Acebo	2 addresses	927141724
info@elbecerril.com		
Acebo	las fuentes de agata	927514413
Acebo	los robles	927514121
info@casalosrobles.com		
Acehuche	2 addresses	927374259
elolivosilguero@hotmail.com		
Alange	la casa azul	924365459
Alcantara	san antonio	927390822
Alcantara	la cañada	927390298
casalacanada@terra.es		
Alcantara	el galapero	927390042
elgalapero@hotmail.com		
Alcantara	la nacencia	927390522
info@lanacencia.com		
Aldea del cano	vía de la plata	927383060
info@crviadelaplata.com		
Aldea del obispo, la	el tenado	927311677
info@eltenado.com		
Aldeacentenera	la coraja	927314129
lacoraja@terra.es		
Aldeanueva de la vera	puerto del emperador	927572540
Alia	el estrecho de la peña	927366289
crestrecho@terra.es / david.duran@terra.es		
Aljucen	la bóveda	690060975
laboveda@crlaboveda.com		
Almoharin	la atalaya	927386351
info@almoharinrural.com		
Arroyomolinos d la vera	la toza	927177549
Atalaya	2 addresses	924125083
comercial@fincaslosllanos.org		
Azuaga	cortijo viña del duco	924890292
jmena@grupo-entorno.com		
Azuaga	la hoya	924890390
correo@hostaljimenez.com		
Azuaga	3 addresses	924890307
Baños de montemayor	la hornera	923428187
Baños de montemayor	viña del baño	923428231
Baños de montemayor	la pesquera	927481330
ramon@lapesquerarural.com		
Barbaño	torreáguila	617457496
torreaguila@aeturex.org		
Barrado	el callejón	927478130
Barrado	los morales	927478154
barradolm@inicia.es		
Benquerencia	sabino alcantara	924776191
Benquerencia de serena	el palomar	924772398
info@casaelpalomar.com		
Berzocana	finca la sierra	669264449
info@fincalasierra.com		
Brozas	la huerta	699354473
lahuertacasarural@yahoo.es		
Cabañas del castillo	la jara de las villuercas	927151009
info@lajaradelasvilluercas.com		
Cabañas del castillo	la peña	927151067
Cabañas del castillo	la costana	927151626
Cabeza del buey	la loma	924600327
Cabezabellosa	el taller	927489044
Cabezabellosa	villa lucía	670627662
Cabezabellosa	carvajal	656978234
casacarvajal@yahoo.es		
Cabezuela del valle	la casa vieja	696516787
Cabezuela del valle	la chinata	927194061
Cabezuela del valle	la cerecera	927472644
info@lacerecera.com		
Cabezuela del valle	los portales	927472601
Caceres	castillo de las seguras	927234725
Caceres	dehesa peña horcada	927216053
pehorcada@csmail.com		
Cachorrilla	casa candido	927140748
casarural@ole.com		
Cadalso	la sierra	659209095
Caminomorisco	la bellua	627900090
casarural@labellua.com		
Caminomorisco	la jareta	657288321
Campillo de llerena	la posada	924770304
Cañamero	los naranjos	927369231
Capilla	la cornicabra	924614478
Carbajo	baldio grande	913105487
Carrascalejo	cancho gordo	661423874
Casar de caceres	la encarnación	927290701
casaencarnacion@terra.es		

Casar de palomero	don romualdo	924270811
Casas del castañar	villaflor	927421448
Casas del castañar info@jerterural.com	5 addresses	927478220
Casas del monte abuela@hervasycomarca.com	la casa de la abuela	678588906
Casas del monte	el balcon	927179055
Casatejada	el botanico	927547325
Castañar de ibor	amanecer	927554730
Castilblanco casarural@loshuertos.com	los huertos	924654398
Castuera sertur@laserena.org	2 addresses	610390793
Castuera	las setecientas	636865915
Ceclavin	el lagar	927393397
Cilleros	la mesonera	646486338
Collado info@vinagrande.com	viña grande	927460308
Collado info@elolivardelejido.com	el olivar del ejido	609575061
Conquista de la sierra reservas@casaruralpizarro.com	pizarro	927312155
Cuacos de yuste lacasona@lacasonadevalfrio.com	la casona de valfrio	927194222
Cuacos de yuste emilio.p.a.@terra.es	colmenarejo	927172210
Cuacos de yuste choncg@hotmail.com	casa la ciega	927172307
Cuacos de yuste verayuste@eresmas.com	la vera de yuste	927172289
Cuacos de yuste casarural@lacasagrandedeyuste.com	la casa grande de yuste	629235333
Cuacos de yuste hosteriacantarranas@hotmail.com	hosteria cantarranas	680435560
Cuacos de yuste caminoyuste@inicia.es	el camino de yuste	927172345
Deleitosa	llano del pino	659962323
Esparragalejo	dehesa la gabrielina	924661242
Fregenal de la sierra	el lucio	924701070
Fresnedoso de ibor	casa grande	927575382
Garganta la olla	el abuelo marciano	927460426
Garganta la olla	parada real	927179605
Gargantilla	la bodega	927484202
Gata casamaire@yahoo.es	casa maire	927672079
Gata info@lasjanonas.com	las jañonas	927672284
Gata jjvaliente@inicia.es	la posada de norberta	927672081
Gata info@zocaillarural.com	zocailla	927672302
Gata elfortin@terra.es	el fortín	689729480
Granja (la)	el miliario	927486161
Guadalupe	molino el batán	927154184
Guadalupe guadaluperural@wanadoo.es	abaceria	927154282
Guadalupe laclara@casarurallaclara.com	la clara	927154067
Guijo de coria	la familia	927449075
Guijo de granadilla ellabriego@yahoo.es	el labriego	927439059
Guijo de santa barbara tormantos@tiscali.es	sierra de tormantos	927560394
Guijo de santa barbara simon.jimenez@casaruralsantabarbara.com	santa barbara	927560424
Guijo de santa barbara casalaabuela@fdg.es	la casa de la abuela	927561008
Helechosa de los montes reserva@elahijondeayuso.com	el ahijon de ayuso	942658318
Helechosa de los montes info@legolacb.com	los montes	924899010
Herguijuela hackenbergd@aol.com	2 addresses	927312160
Herguijuela henri@facilnet.es	santa marta	927319203
Herrera de alcantara dehesadesolana@ari.es	la solana	927491075
Herrera de alcantara agroturismo@losbayones.com	5 addresses	923238185
Hervas casarural@eljardindelconvento.com	el jardín del convento	927481161
Hervas atalaya@hervasycomarca.com	2 addresses	927473414
Hervas	beit shalom	927473508
Hinojal hinojalrural@terra.es	el corralon	927286136
Hinojal hinojalrural@terra.es	la resolana	927286145
Horcajo reservas@extremadurarural.com	el molino	626636198
Hornachos	tita sacramento	924534218

Hornachos	los castillejos	927534067
Hornachos	sierra pinos	924875124
sierrapinos@yahoo.es		
Hornachos	sierra de mampar	924124020
Hoyos	casa del obispo	927514530
Hoyos	casa vieja	927514138
corrago@teleline.es		
Jaraiz de la vera	casa churruca	927170820
casachurruca@laveracasaruralchurruca.com		
Jaraiz de la vera	finca valvellidos	927194143
valvellidos@valvellidos.com		
Jaraiz de la vera	vera yuste	606965484
Jaraiz de la vera	parque puente bolos	659449428
Jarandilla de la vera	el caserio de los 10 cerezos	
927561329		
Jarandilla de la vera	la bodega	659348077
correo@crlabodega.com		
Jerez de los caballeros	la zafrilla	924731031
Jerte	huracás	927470253
huracas@arrakis.es		
Jerte	el cerezal de los sotos	927470429
elcerezaldelossotos@hotmail.com		
Jerte	la sotorriza	927470052
lasotorriza@donbellota.com		
Jerte	el tejo	927470413
reservas@casaruraleltejo.net		
Jerte	la casona	927470313
luisperezcepeda@alojamientorural.com		
La codosera	la jara	924404056
La codosera	la casa grande de adolfo	666281998
info@casaruraladolfo.com		
La garrovilla	huerta los naranjos	924335468
varela@badajoz.dip-badajoz.es		
La parra	cortijo torres	924671708
montobescl@terra.es		
Logrosan	el olivo	927158122
isabelvn@hotmail.com		
Logrosan	el portalon	927360218
info@crelportalon.com		
Losar de la vera	finca los cañejales	927198237
Losar de la vera	la garzona	927570639
reservas@hslagarzona.com		
Madrigal de la vera	antigua fabrica de la luz	609444506
Madrigal de la vera	la puente vieja	927565353
info@lapuentevieja.com		
Madrigal de la vera	alma de gredos	620893697
informacion@almadegredos.com		

Magacela	villasol	699912023
Malpartida de caceres	casa el doncel	927275109
eldoncel@casaeldoncel.com		
Malpartida de plasencia	flor de jara	927459430
reservas@casaruralflordejara.com		
Malpartida de plasencia	la posada de amonaria	927459446
posada@amonaria.com		
Malpartida de plasencia	tia tomasa	696634156
reservas@tiatomasa.com		
Malpartida de plasencia	del corral	927459522
crdelcorral@hotmail.com		
Merida	cortijo de la serrana	924452874
Membrio	turismo rural la nora	927594125
tclaros@airtel.net		
Mirandilla	casa del molinero	658561076
rural@casadelmolinero.com		
Moheda, la	la mohedilla	927140110
lamohedilla@telefonica.net		
Monesterio	la cabra	924517332
Monroy	la bodega del herrador	927280117
labodegadelherrador@yahoo.es		
Montanchez	el fontano	927380173
info@casaruralfontano.com		
Montanchez	balcon de extremadura	927380392
Montanchez	margarita	927380042
maribelfdezgalan@yahoo.es		
Montanchez	el canchalejo	676375500
info@casaruralcanchalejo.com		
Montemolin	el aguila	924510264
info@aventurastentudia.com		
Navaconcejo	el cerrillo	927173276
Navaconcejo	la parra	927173220
laparra@la_parra.com		
Navaconcejo	la tahona	927173654
Navaconcejo	el molino del sol	927470313
luisperezcepeda@alojamientorural.com		
Navaconcejo	el camino	927173453
Navaconcejo	la casa del bosque	927173140
lacasadelbosque@jazzfree.com		
Navaconcejo	casa josefina	927173297
Navaconcejo	la casa blanca	927173202
Navaconcejo	casa bárbara	927173222
unomenos@mundofree.com		
Navaconcejo	los carazos	651375610
Navalvillar de pela	la lozana	924860428
info@lalozana.com		

Location	Name	Phone
Oliva de plasencia	villa caparra	927413010
villacaparra@hispavista.com		
Ovejuela	el tomillar	927674136
siso@ozu.es		
Ovejuela	el chorritero	927674169
chorritero@ozu.es		
Palomero	bellavista	927425588
Pasaron de la vera	los serranos	670824669
chema@ruralis.net		
Pasaron de la vera	el tomillar	927469368
creltomillar@terra.es		
Pasaron de la vera	antigua botica	927469067
pasaron@laantiguabotica.com		
Pasaron de la vera	el rollo	927469174
Pedroso de acim	el postigo	983540695
elpostigocr@telefonica.net		
Pedroso de acim	2 addresses	927192038
candido@arrakis.es		
Peraleda del zaucejo	faica	924636657
Peraleda del zaucejo	casa gabriel	924636744
Pesga (la)	los beltrán	927473432
losbeltran@lashurdes.com		
Piornal	casa verde	927476395
Piornal	2 addresses	927476330
tursmorural@terra.es		
Plasencia	severina	927413539
Plasencia	la umbría	927411485
info@casaruralumbria.com / umbria@terra.es		
Portezuelo	posada pizarro	927302111
Puebla de alcocer	valles de consolacion a	924145039
Puebla de alcocer	la botica	924620315
Puebla de obando	la viña del tío geraldo	924221196
reservas@lavinadetiogeraldo.com		
Rebollar	2 addresses	927471015
crpuriagamellas@hotmail.com		
Retamal de llerena	los nogales	924774005
Riomalo de abajo	la jurdana	927434050
Robledillo de gata	valdarrago	927671035
cristina@unex.es		
Robledillo de gata	luna menguante	927671014
info@luna-rural.com		
Robledillo de gata	cosmopolita	927671048
Robledillo de gata	el pontón	927501797
ponton@constancio.net		
Robledillo de gata	azabal	927671073
Robledillo de gata	cazapolen	927671109
Romangordo	la sartenilla	927576538
sartenilla@sartenilla.com		
Rubiaco	vega vieja	927433069
Salorino	el baldío	927245522
reservas@casaruralelbaldio.com		
Salvaleon	caballería (2)	924121010
turismoruralsalvaleon@yahoo.es		
Salvatierra de barros	el altozano	924698335
Salvatierra de barros	santa lucia	924698070
San martín de trevejo	casa antolina	927510529
marian@casa-antolina.com		
San martín de trevejo	la huerta de valdomingo	927141724
info@elbecerril.com		
San martín de trevejo	casa zoila	927513130
San vicente de alcantara	sierra de san pedro	924410070
info@turismosierrasanpedro.com		
Santa cruz de la sierra	casa del conde	927342243
casadelconde@wanadoo.es		
Sauceda	el rincón de las hurdes	927514061
Segura de leon	la jara y el romero	924259792
Segura de toro	ciudad de verdeoliva	927484162
picutecdv@hotmail.com		
Serradilla	la sierra de monfragüe	927199004
sierramonfrague@terra.es		
Serradilla	la almazara del cristo	927407090
almazara@serradilla.com		
Sierra de fuentes	las avutardas	927201201
info@lasavutardas.com		
Talaván	la breña	927285393
casaruraltalavan@hotmail.com		
Tejeda de tietar	l a vallejera	927194121
juanpedrogiron@gironmendo.com		
Tejeda de tietar	la antigua casa de los pescadores	
927469439		
Tornavacas	antigua posada	608852131
Tornavacas	el puente	927420101
Tornavacas	la escondida	637082515
Torno (el)	el regajo	686092597
elregajo@hotmail.com		
Torno (el)	la solana	927175301
crlasolana@terra.es		
Torre de don miguel	el vínculo	927441451
Torre de santa maría	del obispo	927230088
Torre de santa maría	ruta de las torres	927388660
karmeleeh@hotmail.com		
Torrejon el rubio	posada el arriero	927455050

Torrejon el rubio carvajal@bme.es	la cañada	927455088
Torrejon el rubio crlaserrana@hotmail.com	refugio la serrana	927455159
Torrejon el rubio p_falcon@hotmail.com	peña falcón	927455187
Torremenga lacasona@3imedia.net	la casona	927194145
Trevejo	el corrillo	927513070
Trujillo henri@facilnet.es	2 addresses	927319203
Trujillo	el recuerdo	927319349
Trujillo	los torrejones	927490049
Trujillo	las canteras	609861315
Valdastillas casaruralgarzareal@yahoo.es	garza real	626982784
Valdeobispo	la maya	927456072
Valdeobispo nati_manzano@wanadoo.es	la atalayuela	927180067
Valdetorres	la morera	924368549
Valencia de alcantara casarural@castanar.com	"el castañar iv"	629237753
Valencia de alcantara info@virgencabeza.com	virgen de la cabeza	924251791
Valencia de alcantara jiniebro@hotmail.com	el jiniebro	927584062
Valencia de alcantara informacion@elregato.net	el regato	927491078
Valencia de alcantara saltocaballo@gmx.net	salto de caballo	927580865
Valencia de alcantara	montenuevo	927599021
Valencia de alcantara latoraagroturismo@ya.com	5 addresses	686965445
Valencia de alcantara casarural@castanar.com	el castañar (3)	629237753
Valencia de alcantara casarural@lajiguera.com	la jiguera	927582591
Valverde de la vera elsotanillo@mixmail.com	el sotanillo	927566669
Valverde de la vera casarural@lapicotadevalverde.com	la picota de valverde	649933890
Valverde de leganes losgaitanes@telefonica.net	los gaitanes	924496181
Valverde del fresno info@aantigua.com	a antigua	687825299
Valverde del fresno info@manantioblanco.com	manantio blanco	927510574

Valverde del fresno info@losmontejos.com	los montejos	927510266
Villa del campo	la villa	927448243
Villagarcia de la torre	el hacho	924875681
Villamiel elhornillo@aeturex.org	el hornillo	927193061
Villamiel info@elcabezo.com	el cabezo	927193106
Villamiel	fuente arcada	927193081
Villamiel saltorural@terra.es	el salto	699839290
Villamiel	el parador	927513215
Villanueva de la sierra rafael.lopez.ro@terra.es	evamar	927445272
Villanueva de la sierra casa.de.roman@terra.es	casa de román	696696227
Villanueva de la vera cpozo@fdg.es	la casa del pozo	927566262
Villanueva de la vera 609274870	el balcón de la umbrigüela	
Villanueva de la vera laveritacasarural@hotmail.com	la verita	620077919
Villanueva de la vera info@casaruralentreaguas.com	entreaguas	667525095
Villanueva de la vera atuvera@inicia.es	a tu vera	927198038
Villar de plasencia reservas@casatiaemilia.com	la casa de tia emilia	927489028
Villarreal de san carlos casarural@elcabrerin.com	el cabrerin	927199191
Villarta de los montes balmontes@balmontes.com	balcón de los montes	924641514
Villasbuenas de gata elteso@tiscali.es	el teso	927673046
Villasbuenas de gata donatilacr@lettera.net	casa donatila	927673037

CASAS RURALES / RURAL LODGING

Acebo	corvina	927141785
hrcorvina@hotmail.com		
Alburquerque	los cantos	924141270
Aldeanueva del camino	posada tresmentiras	667620585
hotelrural@tresmentiras.com		
Arroyo de san servan	los pozitos	665992490
Arroyomolinos de la vera		peña del alba
927177516	pdelalba@pdelalba.com	
Baños de montemayor	los postigos	923428117
h.r.lospostigos@terra.es		
Berzocana	real villa de berzocana	927150052
info@hotelrealvilladeberzocana.com		
Bienvenida	la bienvenida	924506648
rusticaelabienvenida@hotmail.com		
Brozas	el vaqueril	927191001
elvaqueril@elvaqueril.com (www.elvaqueril.com)		
Brozas	convento de la luz	927395439
rioconvento@gruporiodehoteles.com		
Cadalso	tres azules	927441414
centrodereposo@tresazules.com		
Caminomorisco	cristania	927435338
Carbajo	baldio grande	927491014
info@baldiogrande.com (www.baldiogrande.com)		
Collado	alcor del roble	927460821
informacion@alcordelroble.com		
Cuacos de yuste	abadía de yuste	927172241
gerencia@abadiadeyuste.com		
Fresnedoso de ibor	los ibores	927575251
Fuente de cantos	la fábrica	924500042
hotel@hrlafabrica.com		
Guadalupe	atalaya	927154226
Guadalupe	posada del rincón	927367114
recepcion@posadadelrincon.com(www.posadadelrincon.		
Guijo de santa barbara	camino real	927561119
caminoreal@casaruralcaminoreal.com		
Jaraicejo	montefragoso	927336189
Jaraiz de la vera	villa xharaiz	927665150
villaxharaiz@villaxharaiz.com		
Jarandilla de la vera	ruta imperial	927561330
info@hotelruralrutaimperial.com		
Jarandilla de la vera	don juan de austria	927560206
hotel@hoteljaranda.com		
Llerena	la fabrica	924500042
hrlafabrica@hrlafabrica.com		

Losar de la vera	antigua casa del heno	927198077
Madroñera	soterraña (2)	927334262
soterrana@soterrana.com		
Merida	el pantano	924140194
navamonte_sa@hotmail.com		
Navaconcejo	xerete	927194240
Olivenza	la coitá del ventoso	659314512
Pasaron de la vera	la casa de pasarón	927469407
pasaron@pasaron.com		
Perales del puerto	don julio	927514651
hrdonjulio@terra.es		
Pinofranqueado	castuo	927674015
www.hotelcastuo.galeon.com		
Santibañez el bajo	ruidioro	927670071
hotelruidioro@terra.es		
Serrejon	el alcaudón	927547600
info@alcaudón.net		
Tejeda de tietar	hojaranzos	927469381
hojaranzos@hotmail.com		
Toril	puerta de monfragüe	927198110
Tornavacas	finca el carpintero	927177089
Torremenga	el turcal	616611116
elturcal@elturcal.com		
Trujillo	viña las torres	927319350
info@vinalastorres.com (www.vinalastorres.com)		
Valencia de alcantara	convento, el	927584129
elconvento@terra.es		
Villanueva de la vera	quinta del castro	616273109
www.quintadelcastro.com		
Villanueva de la vera	el balcon de la vera	659223396
info@elbalcondelavera.com		

Camp sites

Alcantara	puente de alcantara	927390934
recepcion@campingalcantara.com		
Aldeanueva de la vera	yuste	927572522
Aldeanueva del camino	roma	927479132
campingroma@wanadoo.es		
Azuaga	campiña sur	924144074
info@campinasur.com		
Baños de montemayor	cañadas, las	927481126
info@camping-lascanadas.com		
Castañar de ibor	los ibores	927554654
campinglosibores@telefonica.net		
Cuacos de yuste	carlos i	927172092
campingcarlosprimero@telefonica.net		
Garganta (la)	balcón de extremadura	923414538
Gata	sierra de gata	927672168
cgata@turiex.com		
Guadalupe	villuercas-guadalupe, las	927367139
Hervas	pinajarro	927481673
info@campingelpinajarro.com		
Jarandilla de la vera	vera, la	927560611
leo@campinglavera.com		
Jarandilla de la vera	jaranda	927560454
campingjaranda@eresmas.com		
Jerte	valle del jerte	927470127
camping@elvalledeljerte.com		

Losar de la vera	garganta de cuartos	927570727
Losar de la vera	godoy	927570838
Madrigal de la vera	la mata	927565370
info@campimglamata.com		
Madrigal de la vera	alardos	927565066
Malpartida de plasencia	monfragüe	927459233
contacto@campingmonfrague.com		
Merida	merida	924303453
Miajadas	301	927347914
Monesterio	tentudia	924149021
Moraleja	borbollón	927197008
info@campingborbollon.com		
Navaconcejo	rio jerte	927173006
info@campingriojerte.com		
Pinofranqueado	madroños, los	659181797
Pinofranqueado	pino, el	927674141
Plasencia	chopera, la	927416660
campinglachopera@campinglachopera.com		
Riomalo de abajo	riomalo	927434020
riomalo@riomalo.com		
Valverde del fresno	valverde natural	927510026
camping@valverdenatural.com		

ACKNOWLEDGEMENTS

This guide to Extremadura is the fourth title in the Crossbill Guides series of nature travel guides to the major European natural areas. But Extremadura is not just the number four; Extremadura is in a sense where it all started. During an internship, exactly ten years ago at what is now called Global Nature Fund in Torrejón el Rubio, I fell in love with Extremadura. The area is so beautiful and its nature so valuable, that it deserves the attention and affection of the public. Therefore, Crossbill Guides was founded: to bring across the enthusiasm for the natural beauty of areas such as Extremadura and to give insight in the ecological value of them. Naturally, we had to make a guide on Extremadura and I am very happy that we did.

The people of the Crossbill Guides Foundation, which are mentioned in the colophon on page 2, did not produce this guidebook on their own. If it wasn't for the help of several others, this book could never have the quality is has now. We are highly indebted to Tobias Plieninger, who made his expertise on dehesa agriculture and ecosystems available to us and who worked through the entire manuscript to give his suggestions. Henk Strijbosch gave his suggestions regarding the texts on reptiles and amphibians and Francisco Maria Vazquez Pardo helped with the flora section.
For the visual aspects of this guidebook, The Crossbill Guides Foundation also has a number of people to thank. We are very grateful to Chris Braat, who made the excellent habitat and dehesa illustrations especially for this book. We thank our partner organisation, the Saxifraga Foundation, for providing us with excellent photographs again. We also thank Henk Sierdsema for helping to collect photographic material. Finally, we would like to thank the Junta de Extremadura, and particularly Paloma García Cerro, for enabling to produce this guide and providing us with some superb photographs.

Dirk Hilbers,
Crossbill Guides Foundation, January 2006

PICTURE & ILLUSTRATION CREDITS

The following numbers refer to the pages in the book. The letters refer to the position on the page: t for top, b for bottom, l for left and r for right.

Photos

Crossbill Guides / Hilbers, Dirk: cover, 8, 11, 15(b), 16, 17, 18, 19, 20, 21, 22, 26-27, 29, 30, 35(t+m), 36, 37, 39, 40, 42, 47, 48, 49, 50(t), 51(b), 52(t), 54, 55, 57(b), 58, 59, 64, 65, 67, 69, 70, 72, 73, 74, 79, 80, 82, 86, 87, 90, 92, 93, 94, 95, 96, 97, 98, 102, 105, 113(r), 118, 119(t), 121, 122, 123, 124(m), 125, 126, 128, 130, 132, 133, 134, 136, 139, 141, 142, 144, 145, 147, 149, 154, 155, 158, 161, 162, 165, 167, 168, 170, 173, 174, 176, 177, 179, 180, 182, 183(l),

Felix, Rob: 23(b), 44, 45, 51(t), 84, 110-111, 116, 120, 164, 184, 186-187

Hazelhorst, Herman: cover, 53, 66, 109(b)

Junta de Extremadura: 46, 52(b), 57(t), 63, 68, 103(t), 105, 109(b), 113, 115, 156, 157, 183(r)

Saxifraga / Bink, Frits: 124(b)

Saxifraga / Munsterman, Piet: 23(t), 108, 131, 151

Saxifraga / Nijendijk, Jan: 112

Saxifraga / Schelvis, Jaap: 103(b)

Saxifraga / Straaten, Jan van der: 14, 35 (b), 91, 109(t), 117(t)

Saxifraga / Uchelen, Edo van: 117(b), 119(b)

Saxifraga / Winkel, Edwin: 104, 106, 107, 108

Sierdsema, Henk: 8, 15(t), 28, 50(b), 122, 124(t)

Illustrations

Crossbill Guides / Wolter, Horst: all maps and illustrations on p. 88, 89, 100

Braat, Chris: illustrations on p. 24, 32, 33

SPECIES LIST & TRANSLATION

The following list comprises all the species mentioned in this guidebook and gives their scientific, German and Dutch names. Some have an asterisk (*) behind them, indicating an unofficial name. See page 5 for more details.

The Saxifraga and Crossbill Guides Foundations have created a unique picture database on the plant and animal species mentioned in this guide book. You can visit this database either at WWW.CROSSBILLGUIDES.ORG or at WWW.SAXIFRAGA.NL.

Plants

English	Scientific	German	Dutch
Adenocarpus, southern	Adenocarpus telonensis	Mittelmeer-Drüsenginster*	Mediterrane klierbrem*
Adenocarpus, Spanish*	Adenocarpus argyrophyllus	Spanische Drüsenginster*	Spaanse klierbrem*
Alder	Alnus glutinosa	Schwarz-Erle	Zwarte els
Alkanet, large blue	Anchusa azurea	Italienische Ochsenzunge	Italiaanse ossetong
Alkanet, undulate	Anchusa undulata	Wellblättrige Ochsenzunge	Gegolfde ossentong*
Andryala	Andryala integrifolia	Ganzblättrige Andryale	Wolsla
Anemone, palmate	Anemone palmata	Iberische Frühlings-Anemone	Mediterrane gele anemoon*
Artichoke, wild	Cynara cardunculus	Artischocke, Kardone	Wilde artisjok, Kardoen
Ash, narrow-leaved	Fraxinus angustifolia	Schmalblättrige Esche	Smalbladige es
Asparagus, wild	Asparagus sp.	Wilder Spargel	Wilde asperge
Aspen, trembling	Populus tremula	Zitter-Pappel	Ratelpopulier
Asphodel, common	Asphodelus aestivus	Kleinfrüchtiger Affodill	Gewone affodil
Asphodel, hollow-stemmed	Asphodelus fistulosus	Röhriger Affodill	Holle affodil*
Asphodel, white	Asphodelus albus	Weisser Affodill	Witte affodil
Autumn-crocus, Portuguese*	Colchicum lusitanicum	Iberische Zeitlose*	Iberische herfsttijloos
Balm, basterd	Mellitis mellisophyllum	Immenblad	Bijenblad

English	Scientific	German	Dutch
Barley	Hordeum vulgare	Mehrzeilige Gerste	Gerst
Bellflower, rampion	Campanula rapunculus	Rapunzel-Glockenblume	Rapunzelklokje
Bellflower, Spanish spreading*	Campanula patula lusitanica	Lusitanische Wiesen-Glockenblume*	Iberisch weideklokje*
Bindweed, mallow-leaved	Convolvulus althaeoides	Eibischblättrige Winde	Heemstbladige winde
Birch, silver	Betula pendula	Hänge-Birke	Ruwe berk
Birthwort, green-flowered*	Aristolochia paucinervis	Grunblütiges Pfeifenblume*	Groenbloemige pijpbloem*
Bluebell, brown	Dipcadi serotinum	Schweifblatt	Bruine hyacint*
Bluebell, Spanish	Scilla hispanica	Spanisches Hasenglöckchen	Spaanse hyacint
Bramble, elm-leaved	Rubus ulmifolius	Mittelmeer-Brombeere	Koebraam
Broom, common	Cytisus scoparia	Besenginster	Gewone brem
Broom, Piorno*	Cytisus balansae	Piorno-Ginster*	Piornobrem*
Broom, Spanish white	Cytisus multiflorus	Vielblütiger Ginster	Witte brem
Broomrape, branched	Orobanche ramosa	Ästige-Sommerwurz	Hennepvreter
Broomrape, greater	Orobanche rapum-genistae	Ginster-Sommerwurz	Grote bremraap
Bryony, black	Tamus communis	Schmerwurz	Spekwortel
Buckler-fern, broad	Dryopteris dilatata	Breitblättriger Dornfarn	Brede stekelvaren
Buckthorn, alder	Rhamnus frangula	Faulbaum	Sporkenhout
Catchfly, pink*	Silene scabriflora	Farbige Lichtnelke*	Kleurige koekoeksbloem*
Catchfly, small-flowered	Silene gallica	Französisches Lichtnelke	Franse silene
Chamomile, yellow	Anthemis tinctoria	Färber-Hundskamille	Gele kamille
Cherry, wild	Prunus avium	Süss-Kirsche	Zoete kers
Chestnut, sweet	Castanea sativa	Edelkastanie	Tamme kastanje
Cistus, grey-leaved	Cistus albidus	Weissliche Zistrose	Viltig zonneroosje*
Cistus, gum	Cistus ladanifer	Lackzistrose	Kleverig zonneroosje*
Cistus, laurel-leaved	Cistus laurifolius	Lorbeerblättrige Zistrose	Laurierbladig zonneroosje*
Cistus, narrow-leaved	Cistus monspelliensis	Montpellier-Zistrose	Smalbladig zonneroosje*
Cistus, poplar-leaved	Cistus populifolius	Pappelblättrige Zistrose	Populierbladig zonneroosje*
Cistus, Portuguese*	Cistus psilosepalus	Portugiesische Zistrose*	Portugees zonneroosje*
Cistus, sage-leaved	Cistus salvifolius	Salbeiblättriges Zistrose	Saliebladig zonneroosje
Cistus, wrinkle-leaved*	Cistus crispus	Krause Zistrose	Krulzonneroosje*
Clover, star	Trifolium stellatum	Sternklee	Sterklaver
Cowslip	Primula veris	Wiesen-Schlüsselblume	Gulden sleutelbloem
Crucifers	Brassicaceae	Kreuzblütler	Kruisbloemigen
Daffodil, hoop-petticoat	Narcissus bulbocodium	Reifrocknarzisse	Hoepelroknarcis
Daisy, annual	Bellis annua	Einjähriges Gänseblümchen	Eenjarig madelief
Daisy, southern	Bellis sylvestris	Wald-Gänseblümchen	Groot madelief
Dog-rose	Rosa canina	Hundsrose	Hondsroos

English	Scientific	German	Dutch	211
Eucalyptus	Eucalyptus sp.	Eucalyptus	Eucalyptus	
Evax, pygmy	Evax pygmea	Zwerg-Edelweiss	Dwerg edelweiss*	
False-broom, Iberian*	Osyris quadripartita	Iberischer Rutenstrauch*	Iberische valse brem*	
False-broom, white*	Osyris alba	Honigduftender Rutenstrauch	Witte valse brem*	
Fennel, giant	Ferula communis	Riesenfenchel	Reuzenvenkel	
Fern, bracken	Pteridium aquilinum	Adlerfarn	Adelaarsvaren	
Fern, Jersey	Anogramma leptophylla	Nacktfarn	Eenjarige dwergvaren*	
Flax, white	Linum suffruticosum	Strauchiger Lein	Wit vlas*	
Foxglove, Heywood's*	Digitalis heywoodii	Heywoods Fingerhut*	Heywoods vingerhoedskruid*	
Foxglove, pink*	Digitalis thapsi	Iberischer Fingerhut	Iberisch vingerhoedskruid*	
Friar's cowl	Arisarum vulgare	Krummstab	Kromstafaronskelk	
Galactites	Galactites tomentosa	Milchfleckdistel	Galactites*	
Garlic, rosy	Allium roseum	Rosen-Lauch	Roze look	
Gentian, Gredos*	Gentiana boryi	Gredos-Enzian*	Gredos gentiaan*	
Germander, shrubby	Teucrium fruticans	Strauch-Gamander	Struikgamander	
Gladiolus, Italian	Gladiolus segetum	Saat-Siegwurz	Italiaanse gladiool*	
Gladiolus, wild	Gladiolus illyricus	Illyrische Siegwurz	Illyrische gladiool*	
Gorses	Ulex sp.	Stechginster	Gaspeldoorn	
Grape-vine	Vitis vinifera	Wilde Weinrebe	Wilde wijnstok	
Greenweed, spiny*	Genista hirsuta	Behaarter Ginster	Behaarde brem*	
Greenweed, winged*	Genista tridentata	Geflügelter Ginster*	Gevleugelde brem*	
Gromwell, shrubby	Lithodora fruticosa	Strauch-Steinsame*	Struikparelzaad*	
Hackberry, Mediterranean	Celtis australis	Zürgelbaum	Europese netelboom	
Hard-fern	Blechnum spicant	Rippenfarn	Dubbelloof	
Hawkbeards	Crepis sp.	Pippau	Streepzaad	
Hawthorn	Crataegus monogyna	Eingriffeliger Weissdorn	Eenstijlige meidoorn	
Heath, Portuguese	Erica lusitanica	Portugiesische Heide	Portugese hei*	
Heath, Spanish	Erica australis	Südliche heide	Spaanse hei*	
Heath, tree	Erica arborea	Baumheide	Boomhei	
Heath, umbel-flowered*	Erica umbellata	Schirmheide*	Schermdophei*	
Heather	Calluna vulgaris	Besenheide	Struikhei	
Helleborine, narrow-leaved	Cephalanthera longifolia	Schwertblättriges Waldvögelein	Wit bosvogeltje	
Helleborine, red	Cephalanthera rubra	Rotes Waldvögelein	Rood bosvogeltje	
Hyacinth, tassel	Muscari comosum	Schopf-Traubenhyazinthe	Kuifhyacint	
Hypocist	Cytinus hypocistis	Zistrosenwürger	Gele hypocist	
Iris, Spanish	Iris xiphium	Spanishe Schwertlilie	Spaanse lis	
Iris, winter*	Iris planifolia	Flachblättrige Iris	Winter iris*	
Jasmine, wild	Jasminum fruticans	Strauch-Jasmin	Struikjasmijn	

English	Scientific	German	Dutch
Jerusalem-sage, Iberian*	Phlomis lychnitis	Filziges Brandkraut	Viltbrandkruid*
Juniper, common	Juniperus communis	Gewöhnlicher Wacholder	Jeneverbes
Juniper, prickly	Juniperus oxycedrus	Stechwacholder	Spaanse jeneverbes
Lady's-tresses, summer	Spiranthes aestivalis	Sommer-Drehwurz	Zomerschroeforchis
Laurel, Portuguese	Prunus lusitanica	Portugiesischer Lorbeer	Portugese laurierkers
Laurustinus	Viburnum tinus	Immergrüner Schneeball	Altijdgroene sneeuwbal
Lavender, French	Lavandula stoechas	Schopflavendel	Kuiflavendel
Lentisc	Pistacia lentiscus	Mastixstrauch	Mastiekstruik
Lily, Kerry	Simethis planifolia	Westlicher Lilie*	Westelijke lelie*
Lords-and-ladies	Arum maculatum	Gefleckter Aronstab	Gevlekte aronskelk
Lucerne	Medicago sativa	Luzerne	Luzerne
Lupin, narrow-leaved	Lupinus angustifolius	Schmallblättrige Lupine	Blauwe lupine
Lupin, Spanish*	Lupinus hispanicus	Spanische Lupine*	Spaanse lupine*
Lupin, yellow	Lupinus luteus	Gelbe Lupine	Gele lupine
Maple, Montpellier	Acer monspessulanum	Französischer Ahorn	Franse esdoorn
Marigold, corn	Chrysanthemum segetum	Saat-Wucherblume	Gele ganzenbloem
Medicks	Medicago sp.	Schneckenklee	Rupsklaver
Merendera	Colchicum pyrenaicum	Pyrenäen-Merendera	Pyrenese Stijlloos
Mezereon, Mediterranean	Daphne gnidium	Immergrüner Seidelbast	Herfstpeperboompje*
Milkvetch, Lusitanian	Astragalus lusitanica	Lusitanischer tragant	Reuzenhokjespeul*
Milkwort, small-leaved*	Polygala microphylla	Schmallblättrige Kreuzblume*	Smalbladige vleugeltjesbloem*
Narcissus, autumn	Narcissus serotinus	Spätblühende Narzisse	Herfstnarcis*
Narcissus, Cantabrian	Narcissus cantabricus	Cantabrische Narzisse*	Cantabrische narcis*
Narcissus, Fernandes's*	Narcissus fernandesii	Fernandes' Narzisse*	Fernandes' narcis*
Narcissus, palid*	Narcissus pallidulus	Blass-Narzisse*	Bleke narcis*
Navelwort	Umbilicus rupestris	Felsen-Nabelkraut	Rotsnavelkruid
Nut, Barbary	Gynandriris sisyrinchium	Mittagsschwertlilie	Dwergiris
Oak, cork	Quercus suber	Korkeiche	Kurkeik
Oak, holm	Quercus (ilex) rotundifolia	Steineiche	Steeneik
Oak, lusitanian	Quercus faginea	Portugiesische Eiche	Portugese eik
Oak, Pyrenean	Quercus pyrenaica	Pyrenäeneiche	Pyreneese eik
Oat	Avena sativa	Saat-Hafer	Haver
Olive, false	Phillyrea angustifolia	Schmalblättrige Steinlinde	Smalbladige steenlinde
Olive, wild	Olea europea	Ölbaum	Wilde olijfboom
Orchid, bee	Ophrys apifera	Bienen-Ragwurz	Bijenorchis
Orchid, bug	Orchis coriophora	Wanzen-Knabenkraut	Wantsenorchis
Orchid, bumblebee	Ophrys bombyliflora	Drohnen-Ragwurz	Weidehommelorchis
Orchid, butterfly	Orchis papilionacea	Schmetterlings-Knabenkraut	Vlinderorchis

SPECIES LIST & TRANSLATION

English	Scientific	German	Dutch
Orchid, Champagne	Orchis champagneuxii	Dreiknolliges Knabenkraut	Blesharlekijn
Orchid, dense-flowered	Neottianthe maculata	Gefleckte Keuschorchis	Nonnetjesorchis
Orchid, Dyris*	Ophrys dyris	Marokkanische Ragwurz	Dyris orchis*
Orchid, early purple	Orchis mascula	Männliches Knabenkraut	Mannetjesorchis
Orchid, giant	Barlia robertiana	Roberts Mastorchis	Hyacinthorchis
Orchid, green tongue*	Serapias perez-chiscanoi	Grunblütiges Zungenstendel*	Groene tongorchis*
Orchid, green-winged	Orchis morio	Kleines Knabenkraut	Harlekijn
Orchid, heart-flowered tongue	Serapias cordigera	Herzförmiger Zungenstendel	Brede tongorchis
Orchid, Lange's	Orchis langei	Spanisches Knabenkraut	IJle mannetjesorchis
Orchid, lax-flowered	Orchis laxiflora	Lockerblütiges Knabenkraut	IJle moerasorchis
Orchid, long-lipped tongue	Serapias vomeracea	Pflugschar Zungenstendel	Lange tongorchis
Orchid, man	Aceras antropophorum	Fratzenorchis	Poppenorchis
Orchid, milky	Orchis lactea	Milchweisses Knabenkraut	Maskerorchis
Orchid, mirror	Ophrys speculum	Spiegel-Ragwurz	Spiegelorchis
Orchid, naked-man	Orchis italica	Italienisches Knabenkraut	Italiaanse orchis
Orchid, pyramidal	Anacamptis pyramidalis	Hundswurz	Hondskruid
Orchid, sawfly	Ophrys tenthredinifera	Wespen-Ragwurz	Wolzweverorchis
Orchid, Sicilian	Dactylorhiza markusii	Sizilianisches Knabenkraut	Siciliaanse orchis*
Orchid, small-flowered tongue	Serapias parviflora	Kleinblütiger Zungenstendel	Kleine tongorchis
Orchid, sombre bee	Ophrys fusca	Braune Ragwurz	Bruine orchis
Orchid, southern early purple*	Orchis olbiensis	Hyères-Knabenkraut	Kleine mannetjesorchis
Orchid, tongue	Serapias lingua	Einschwieliger Zugenstendel	Gewone tongorchis
Orchid, violet bird's-nest	Limodorum abortivum	Violetter Dingel	Paarse aspergeorchis
Orchid, woodcock	Ophrys scolopax	Schnepfen-Ragwurz	Snippenorchis
Orchid, yellow bee	Ophrys lutea	Gelbe Ragwurz	Gele orchis
Oregano, Spanish	Thymbra capitata	Kopfiger Thymian	Spaanse oregano*
Pear, Spanish wild*	Pyrus bourgeana	Spanischer Wilder Birnbaum*	Spaanse wilde peer*
Peony, western	Paeonia broteroi	Westlicher Pfingstrose*	Westelijke pioenroos*
Pine, maritime	Pinus pinaster	Strandkiefer	Zeeden
Pine, scots	Pinus sylvestris	Waldkiefer	Grove den
Pine, umbrella	Pinus pinea	Pinie	Parasolden
Poplar, black	Populus nigra	Schwarz-Pappel	Zwarte populier
Poplar, grey	Populus x canescens	Grau-Pappel	Grauwe abeel
Reed	Phragmites australis	Schilfrohr	Riet
Retama	Retama sphaerocarpa	Retama-Ginster	Retamabrem*
Rockrose, orache-leaved*	Halimium atriplicifolium	Melde-Blättriges Sonnenröschen*	Meldebladig zonneroosje*
Rockrose, spotted	Tuberaria guttata	Geflecktes Sonnenröschen	Gevlekt zonneroosje

SPECIES LIST & TRANSLATION

English	Scientific	German	Dutch
Rose, evergreen	Rosa sempervirens	Immergrüne Rose	Groenblijvende roos
Rosemary	Rosmarinus officinalis	Rosmarin	Rozemarijn
Sand-crocus, large-flowered	Romulea bulbocodium	Grossblütiger Scheinkrokus	Grootbloemige schijnkrokus*
Sand-spurrey, purple	Spergularia purpurea	Purpur-Spärkling*	Paarse schijnspurrie
Selaginella, Mediterranean	Selaginella denticulata	Gezähnter Moosfarn	Mediterrane selaginella*
Service-tree, wild	Sorbus torminalis	Elsbeere	Elsbes
Sheep's-bit	Jasione montana	Berg-Sandglöckchen	Zandblauwtje
Sheep's-bit, dwarf*	Jasione crispa	Krauses Sandglöckchen	Dwergzandblauwtje*
Shield-fern, soft	Polystichum setiferum	Borstiger Schildfarn	Zachte naaldvaren
Smilax	Smilax aspera	Stechwinde	Steekwinde
Snakeshead	Fritillaria lusitanica	Portugiesische Schachblume	Iberische kievitsbloem
Snake's-tongue	Biarum arundanum	Schlangenzunge*	Slangentong*
Snapdragon, Gredos'*	Antirrhinum grossi	Gredos Löwenmaul	Gredos Leeuwenbek*
Snowflake, autumn	Leucojum autumnale	Herbst-Knotenblume	Herfstklokje
Solomon's-seal, angular	Polygonatum odoratum	Wohlriechende Weisswurz	Welriekende salomonszegel
Spleenwort, Irish	Asplenium onopteris	Spitziger Streifenfarn	Spitse streepvaren*
Spleenwort, southern*	Asplenium petrarchae	Südliche Streifenfarn*	Zuidelijke streepvaren*
Spurge, red-flowered*	Euphorbia broteroi	Rotblütiges Wolfsmilch*	Roodbloemige wolfsmelk*
Squill, autumn	Scilla autumnalis	Herbst-Blaustern	Herfststerhyacint
Squill, sea	Urginea maritima	Meerzwiebel	Zeeui
Star-of-Bethlehem	Ornithogalum umbellatum	Dolden-Milchstern	Gewone vogelmelk
Steppe-edelweiss, globe-flowered	Paronychia capitata	Kopfige Mauermiere*	Ronde steppe-edelweiss*
Stork's bill, common	Erodium cicutarium	Gewöhnlicher Reiherschnabel	Gewone reigersbek
Strawberry tree	Arbutus unedo	Erdbeerbaum	Aardbeiboom
Sundew, Portuguese	Drosophyllum lusitanicum	Taublatt	Portugese zonnendauw
Sundew, round-leaved	Drosera rotundifolia	Rundblättriger Sonnentau	Ronde zonnendauw
Tamujo*	Securinega tinctoria	Tamujo*	Tamujo*
Thistle, golden	Scolymus hispanicus	Spanische Golddistel	Spaanse gouddistel
Thrift	Armeria sp.	Grasnelke	Engels gras
Thyme, mastic	Thymus mastichina	Mastix-Thymian	Spaanse marjolein
Thyme, Spanish	Thymus zygis	Spanischer Thymian	Spaanse tijm*
Thyme, wild	Thymus sp.	Thymian	Tijm
Toadflax, red	Linaria aeruginea	Dunkelblütiges Leinkraut	Rode leeuwenbek*
Tolpis	Tolpis barbata	Christusauge	Tolpis*
Tulip, wild	Tulipa australis	Südliche Tulpe	Zuidelijke tulp
Turpentine tree	Pistacia terebinthus	Terpentin-Pistazie	Terpentijnboom
Viper's bugloss, Portuguese	Echium lusitanicum	Portugiesische Natterkopf	Portugees slangenkruid*

English	Scientific	German	Dutch
Viper's bugloss, purple	Echium plantagineum	Wegerichblättriger Natterkopf	Weegbreeslangenkruid
Water-crowfoot, common	Ranunculus aquatilis	Wasserhahnenfuss	Fijne waterranonkel
Wheat	Triticum aestivum	Saat-Weizen	Tarwe
Whitebeam, broad-leaved	Sorbus latifolia	Breitblättrige Mehlbeere	Breedbladige lijsterbes
Yew	Taxus baccata	Eibe	Taxus

Mammals

English	Scientific	German	Dutch
Badger	Meles meles	Dachs	Das
Boar, wild	Sus scrofa	Wildschwein	Wild zwijn
Cat, wild	Felis silvestris	Wildkatze	Wilde kat
Deer, red	Cervus elaphus	Rothirsch	Edelhert
Deer, roe	Capreolus capreolus	Reh	Ree
Desman, Pyrenean	Galemys pyrenaicus	Pyrenäen-Desman	Pyreneese desman
Dormice, garden	Eliomys quercinus	Gartenschläfer	Eikelmuis
Fox, red	Vulpes vulpes	Rotfuchs	Vos
Genet	Genetta genetta	Ginsterkatze	Genetkat
Hare, Iberian	Lepus granatensis	Iberische Hase	Iberische haas
Ibex, Iberian	Capra pyrenaica victoriae	Iberischen Steinbock	Gredossteenbok
Lynx, Iberian	Lynx pardinus	Pardelluchs	Pardellynx, Iberische lynx
Marten	Martes sp.	Marder	Marter
Mongoose, Egyptian	Herpestes ichneumon	Ichneumon	Mangoest
Otter	Lutra lutra	Fischotter	Otter
Rabbit	Oryctolagus cuniculus	Wildkaninchen	Konijn
Wolf	Canis lupus	Wolf	Wolf

Birds´

English	Scientific	German	Dutch
Bee-eater	Merops apiaster	Bienenfresser	Bijeneter
Bittern, little	Ixobrychus minutus	Zwergdommel	Woudaapje
Blackbird	Turdus merula	Amsel	Merel
Blackcap	Sylvia atricapilla	Mönchsgrasmücke	Zwartkop
Bluethroat	Luscinia svecica	Blaukehlchen	Blauwborst
Bunting, cirl	Emberiza cirlus	Zaunammer	Cirlgors
Bunting, corn	Miliaria calandra	Grauammer	Grauwe gors
Bunting, hortolan	Emberiza hortelana	Hortolan	Ortolaan
Bunting, rock	Emberiza cia	Zippammer	Grijze gors
Bustard, great	Otis tarda	Grosstrappe	Grote trap
Bustard, little	Tetrax tetrax	Zwergtrappe	Kleine trap
Chaffinch	Fringilla coelebs	Buchfink	Vink
Chough, red-billed	Pyrrhocorax pyrrhocorax	Alpenkrähe	Alpenkraai
Cormorant	Phalacrocorax carbo	Kormoran	Aalscholver
Crane	Grus grus	Kranich	Kraanvogel
Cuckoo, common	Cuculus canorus	Kuckuck	Koekoek
Cuckoo, great spotted	Clamator glandarius	Häherkuckuck `	Kuifkoekoek
Curlew, stone	Burhinus oedicnemus	Triel	Griel
Dipper	Cinclus cinclus	Wasseramsel	Waterspreeuw
Dotterel	Charadrius morinellus	Mornellregenpfeifer	Morinelplevier
Dove, rock	Columba livia	Felsentaube	Rotsduif
Dove, stock	Columba oenas	Hohltaube	Holenduif
Eagle, Bonelli's	Hieraaetus fasciatus	Habichtsadler	Havikarend
Eagle, booted	Hieraaetus pennatus	Zwergadler	Dwergarend
Eagle, golden	Aquila chrysaetos	Steinadler	Steenarend
Eagle, short-toed	Circaetus gallicus	Schlangenadler	Slangenarend
Eagle, Spanish imperial	Aquila adalberti	Spanischer Kaiseradler	Spaanse keizerarend
Egret, cattle	Bubulcus ibis	Kuhreiher	Koereiger
Egret, little	Egretta garzetta	Seidenreiher	Kleine zilverreiger
Falcon, peregrine	Falco peregrinus	Wanderfalke	Slechtvalk
Finch, trumpeter	Bucanetes githagineus	Wüstengimpel	Woestijnvink
Flycatcher, pied	Ficedula hypoleuca	Trauerschnäpper	Bonte vliegenvanger
Flycatcher, spotted	Muscicapa striata	Grauschnäpper	Grauwe vliegenvanger
Gallinule, purple	Porphyrio porphyrio	Purpurhuhn	Purperkoet
Goldfinch	Carduelis carduelis	Distelfink	Putter
Grebe, great crested	Podiceps cristatus	Haubentaucher	Fuut

English	Scientific	German	Dutch
Grebe, little	Tachybaptus ruficollis	Zwergtaucher	Dodaars
Greenfinch	Carduelis chloris	Grünling	Groenling
Gulls	Lariidae	Möwe	Meeuwen
Harrier, marsh	Circus aeruginosus	Rohrweihe	Bruine kiekendief
Harrier, Montagu's	Circus pygargus	Wiesenweihe	Grauwe kiekendief
Heron, grey	Ardea cinerea	Graureiher	Blauwe reiger
Heron, night	Nycticorax nycticorax	Nachtreiher	Kwak
Heron, purple	Ardea purpurea	Purpurreiher	Purperreiger
Honey-buzzard	Pernis apivorus	Wespenbussard	Wespendief
Hoopoe	Upupa epops	Wiedehopf	Hop
Jackdaw	Corvus monedula	Dohle	Kauw
Jay	Garrulus glandarius	Eichelhäher	Gaai
Kestrel, common	Falco tinnunculus	Turmfalke	Torenvalk
Kestrel, lesser	Falco naumanni	Rötelfalke	Kleine torenvalk
Kingfisher	Alcedo atthis	Eisvogel	IJsvogel
Kite, black	Milvus migrans	Schwarzmilan	Zwarte wouw
Kite, black-shouldered	Elanus caeruleus	Gleitaar	Grijze wouw
Kite, red	Milvus milvus	Rotmilan	Rode wouw
Lapwing	Vanellus vanellus	Kiebitz	Kievit
Lark, calandra	Melanocorypha calandra	Kalanderlerche	Kalanderleeuwerik
Lark, crested	Galerida cristata	Haubenlerche	Kuifleeuwerik
Lark, Dupont's	Chersophilus duponti	Dupontlerche	Duponts leeuwerik
Lark, short-toed	Calandrella brachydactyla	Kurzzehenlerche	Kortteenleeuwerik
Lark, sky	Alauda arvensis	Feldlerche	Veldleeuwerik
Lark, thekla	Galerida theklae	Theklalerche	Theklaleeuwerik
Lark, wood	Lullula arborea	Heidelerche	Boomleeuwerik
Magpie, azure-winged	Cyanopica cyana	Blauelster	Blauwe ekster
Martin, crag	Ptyonoprogne rupestris	Felsenschwalbe	Rotszwaluw
Martin, house	Delichon urbica	Mehlschwalbe	Huiszwaluw
Merlin	Falco columbarius	Merlin	Smelleken
Nightingale, rufous	Luscinia megarhynchos	Nachtigall	Nachtegaal
Nightjar, red-necked	Caprimulgus ruficollis	Rothals-Ziegenmelker	Moorse nachtzwaluw
Nuthatch	Sitta europaea	Kleiber	Boomklever
Owl, barn	Tyto alba	Schleiereule	Kerkuil
Owl, eagle	Bubo bubo	Uhu	Oehoe
Owl, little	Athene noctua	Steinkauz	Steenuil
Owl, scops	Otus scops	Zwergohreule	Dwergooruil
Partridge, red-legged	Alectoris rufa	Rothuhn	Rode patrijs

SPECIES LIST & TRANSLATION

English	Scientific	German	Dutch
Pigeon, wood	Columba palumbus	Ringeltaube	Houtduif
Pipit, meadow	Anthus pratensis	Wiesenpieper	Graspieper
Plover, golden	Pluvialis apricaria	Goldregenpfeifer	Goudplevier
Plover, little ringed	Charadrius dubius	Flussregenpfeifer	Kleine plevier
Pochard, red-crested	Netta rufina	Kolbenente	Krooneend
Pratincole, collared	Glareola pratincola	Rotflügel-Brachschwalbe	Vorkstaartplevier
Raven	Corvus corax	Kolkrabe	Raaf
Redstart, black	Phoenicurus ochruros	Hausrotschwanz	Zwarte roodstaart
Robin	Erithacus rubecula	Rotkehlchen	Roodborst
Rock thrush	Monticola saxatilis	Steinrötel	Rode rotslijster
Rock thrush, blue	Monticola solitarius	Blaumerle	Blauwe rotslijster
Roller	Coracias garrulus	Blauracke	Scharrelaar
Sandgrouse, black-bellied	Pterocles orientalis	Sandflughuhn	Zwartbuikzandhoen
Sandgrouse, pin-tailed	Pterocles alchata	Spiessflughuhn	Witbuikzandhoen
Sandpiper, common	Actitis hypoleucos	Flussuferläufer	Oeverloper
Serin, European	Serinus serinus	Girlitz	Europese kanarie
Shrike, lesser grey	Lanius minor	Schwarzstirnwürger	Kleine klapekster
Shrike, southern grey	Lanius meridionalis	Südlicher Raubwürger	Zuidelijke klapekster
Shrike, woodchat	Lanius senator	Rotkopfwürger	Roodkopklauwier
Sparrow, house	Passer domesticus	Haussperling	Huismus
Sparrow, rock	Petronia petronia	Steinsperling	Rotsmus
Sparrow, Spanish	Passer hispaniolensis	Weidensperling	Spaanse mus
Starling, spotless	Sturnus unicolor	Einfarbstar	Zwarte spreeuw
Stilt, black-winged	Himantopus himantopus	Stelzenläufer	Steltkluut
Stonechat	Saxicola torquata	Schwarzkehlchen	Roodborsttapuit
Stork, black	Ciconia nigra	Schwarzstorch	Zwarte ooievaar
Stork, white	Ciconia ciconia	Weissstorch	Ooievaar
Swallow, barn	Hirundo rustica	Rauchschwalbe	Boerenzwaluw
Swallow, red-rumped	Hirundo daurica	Rötelschwalbe	Roodstuitzwaluw
Swift, Alpine	Apus melba	Alpensegler	Alpengierzwaluw
Swift, common	Apus apus	Mauersegler	Gierzwaluw
Swift, pallid	Apus pallidus	Fahlsegler	Vale gierzwaluw
Swift, white-rumped	Apus caffer	Kaffernsegler	Kaffergierzwaluw
Teal, common	Anas crecca	Krickente	Wintertaling
Tern, little	Sterna albifrons	Zwergseeschwalbe	Dwergstern
Thrush, mistle	Turdus viscivorus	Misteldrossel	Grote lijster
Thrush, song	Turdus philomelos	Singdrossel	Zanglijster
Tit, blue	Parus caeruleus	Blaumeise	Pimpelmees

SPECIES LIST & TRANSLATION

English	Scientific	German	Dutch
Tit, great	Parus major	Kohlmeise	Koolmees
Tit, long-tailed	Aegithalos caudatus	Schwanzmeise	Staartmees
Treecreeper, short-toed	Certhia brachydactyla	Gartenbaumläufer	Boomkruiper
Vulture, black	Aegypius monachus	Mönchsgeier	Monniksgier
Vulture, Egyptian	Neophron percnopterus	Schmutzgeier	Aasgier
Vulture, griffon	Gyps fulvus	Gänsegeier	Vale gier
Wagtail, grey	Motacilla cinerea	Gebirgsstelze	Grote gele kwikstaart
Wagtail, white	Motacilla alba	Bachstelze	Witte kwikstaart
Wallcreeper	Tichodroma muraria	Mauerläufer	Rotskruiper
Warbler, Bonelli's	Phylloscopus bonelli	Berglaubsänger	Bergfluiter
Warbler, Cetti's	Cettia cetti	Seidensänger	Cetti's zanger
Warbler, Dartford	Sylvia undata	Provencegrasmücke	Provençaalse grasmus
Warbler, fan-tailed	Cisticola juncidis	Cistensänger	Graszanger
Warbler, great reed	Acrocephalus arundinaceus	Drosselrohrsänger	Grote karekiet
Warbler, melodious	Hippolais polyglotta	Orpheusspötter	Orpheusspotvogel
Warbler, olivaceous	Hippolais pallida	Blassspötter	Vale spotvogel
Warbler, Orphean	Sylvia hortensis	Orpheusgrasmücke	Orpheusgrasmus
Warbler, Sardinian	Sylvia melanocephala	Samtkopf-Grasmücke	Kleine zwartkop
Warbler, Savi's	Locustella luscinioides	Rohrschwirl	Snor
Warbler, subalpine	Sylvia cantillans	Weissbart-Grasmücke	Baardgrasmus
Wheatear, black	Oenanthe leucura	Trauersteinschmätzer	Zwarte tapuit
Wheatear, black-eared	Oenanthe hispanica	Mittelmeer-Steinschmätzer	Blonde tapuit
Wheatear, northern	Oenanthe oenanthe	Steinschmätzer	Tapuit
Wigeon	Anas penelope	Pfeifente	Smient
Woodpecker, great spotted	Dendrocopos major	Buntspecht	Grote bonte specht
Wryneck	Jynx torquilla	Wendehals	Draaihals

SPECIES LIST & TRANSLATION

Reptiles and Amphibians

English	Scientific	German	Dutch
Frog, Iberian	Rana iberica	Spanischer Frosch	Iberische beekkikker
Frog, Iberian painted	Discoglossus galganoi	Iberischer Scheibenzüngler	West-Iberische schijftongkikker
Frog, Iberian parsley	Pelodytes ibericus	Iberischer Schlammtaucher	Iberische groengestipte kikker
Frog, Perez's	Rana perezi	Spanischer Wasserfrosch	Iberische meerkikker
Gecko, Moorish	Tarentola mauretanica	Maurischer Gecko	Muurgekko
Gecko, Turkish	Hemidactylus turcicus	Europäischer Halbfinger	Europese tjiktjak
Lizard, common wall	Podarcis muralis	Mauereidechse	Muurhagedis
Lizard, Iberian rock	Lacerta monticola	Iberische Gebirgseidechse	Iberische berghagedis
Lizard, Iberian wall	Podarcis hispanica	Spanische mauereidechse	Spaanse muurhagedis
Lizard, ocellated	Lacerta lepida	Perleidechse	Parelhagedis
Lizard, Schreiber's green	Lacerta schreiberi	Iberische Smaragdeidechse	Iberische smaragdhagedis
Lizard, spiny-footed	Acanthodactylus erythrurus	Europäischer Fransenfinger	Franjeteenhagedis
Lizard, worm	Blanus cinereus	Maurische Netzwühle	Moorse wormhagedis
Newt, Bosca's	Triturus boscai	Spanischer Wassermolch	Iberische watersalamander
Newt, southern marbled	Triturus pygmaeus	Zwergmarmormolch	Dwergmarmersalamander
Psammodromus, large	Psammodromus algirus	Algirischer Sandläufer	Algerijnse zandloper
Psammodromus, Spanish	Psammodromus hispanicus	Spanischer Sandläufer	Spaanse zandloper
Salamander, fire	Salamandra salamandra	Feuersalamander	Vuursalamander
Salamander, sharp-ribbed	Pleurodeles waltl	Spanischer Rippenmolch	Ribbensalamander
Skink, Bedriaga's	Chalcides bedriagai	Iberischer Walzenskink	Iberische skink
Skink, three-toed	Chalcides chalcides	Erzschleiche	Hazelskink
Snake, false smooth	Macroprotodon cucullatus	Kapuzennatter	Mutsslang
Snake, grass	Natrix natrix	Ringelnatter	Ringslang
Snake, horseshoe whip	Coluber hippocrepis	Hufeisennatter	Hoefijzerslang
Snake, ladder	Elaphe scalaris	Treppennatter	Trapslang
Snake, Montpellier	Malpolon monspessulanus	Eidechsennatter	Hagedisslang
Snake, southern smooth	Coronella girondica	Girondische Glattnatter	Girondische gladde slang
Snake, viperine	Natrix maura	Vipernatter	Adderringslang
Spadefoot, western	Pelobates cultripes	Spanischer Messerfuss	Iberische knoflookpad
Terrapin, European pond	Emys orbicularis	Europäische Sumpfschildkröte	Europese moerasschildpad
Terrapin, stripe-necked	Mauremys leprosa	Spanische Wasserschildkröte	Moorse beekschildpad
Toad, common	Bufo bufo	Erdkröte	Gewone pad
Toad, Iberian midwife	Alytes cisternasii	Iberische Geburtshelferkröte	Iberische vroedmeesterpad
Toad, midwife	Alytes obstetricans	Geburtshelferkröte	Vroedmeesterpad
Toad, natterjack	Bufo calamita	Kreuzkröte	Rugstreeppad
Treefrog, stripeless	Hyla meridionalis	Mittelmeer-Laubfrosch	Mediterrane boomkikker

SPECIES LIST & TRANSLATION

English	Scientific	German	Dutch
Viper, Lataste's	Vipera latasti	Stülpnasenotter	Wipneusadder
Worm, slow	Anguis fragilis	Blindschleiche	Hazelworm

Invertebrates

English	Scientific	German	Dutch
Admiral, southern white	Limenitis reducta	Blauschwarzer Eisvogel	Blauwe ijsvogelvlinder
Argus, mountain	Aricia artaxerxes	Grosser Sonnenröschen-Bläuling	Vals bruin blauwtje
Beauty, Camberwell	Nymphalis antiopa	Trauermantel	Rouwmantel
Blue, Lang's short-tailed	Leptotes pirithous	Kleiner Wander-Bläuling	Klein tijgerblauwtje
Blue, mazarine	Polyommatus semiargus	Rotklee-Bläuling	Klaverblauwtje
Blue, silver-studded	Plebeius argus	Geissklee-Bläulling	Heideblauwtje
Brimstone	Gonepteryx rhamni	Zitronenfalter	Citroentje
Brown, large wall	Lasiommata maera	Braunauge	Rotsvlinder
Burnet companion	Euclidia glyphica	Braune Tageule	Bruine daguil
Butterfly, nettle-tree	Libythea celtis	Zürgelbaum-Schnauzenfalter	Snuitvlinder
Cardinal	Argynnis pandora	Kardinal	Kardinaalsmantel
Centipedes	Chilopoda	Hundertfüssler	Duizendpoten
Cicada, red	Tibicina haematodes	Blutaderzikade	Rode cicade*
Cleopatra	Gonepteryx cleopatra	Mittelmeer-Zitronenfalter	Cleopatra
Copper, scarce	Lycaena virgaureae	Dukatenfalter	Morgenrood
Copper, small	Lycaena phlaeas	Kleiner Feuerfalter	Kleine vuurvlinder
Festoon, Spanish	Zerynthia rumina	Spanischer Osterluzeifalter	Spaanse pijpbloemvlinder
Fritillary, dark green	Argynnis aglaja	Grosser Perlmutterfalter	Grote parelmoervlinder
Fritillary, meadow	Melitaea parthenoides	Westlicher Scheckenfalter	Westelijke parelmoervlinder
Fritillary, niobe	Argynnis niobe	Stiefmütterchen-Perlmutterfalter	Duinparelmoervlinder
Fritillary, silver-washed	Argynnis paphia	Kaisermantel	Keizersmantel
Fritillary, small-pearl-bordered	Boloria selene	Braunfleckiger Perlmutterfalter	Zilveren maan
Grasshoppers	Orthoptera	Heuschrecken	Sprinkhanen
Hairstreak, ilex	Satyrium ilicis	Brauner Eichen-Zipfelfalter	Bruine eikenpage
Hairstreak, Spanish purple	Laeosopis roboris	Spanischer Blauer Zipfelfalter	Essenpage
Heath, dusky	Coenonympha dorus	Dorus Wiesenvögelchen	Bleek hooibeestje
Heath, pearly	Coenonympha arcania	Weissbindiges Wiesenvögelchen	Tweekleurig hooibeestje

Locust, Moroccan	Dociostaurus maroccanus	Marokkanische Wanderheuschrecke	Marokkaanse sprinkhaan
Oil-beetle, red-striped	Meloe majalis	Maiwurmkäfer / Ölkäfer	Roodgestreepte oliekever*
Orange-tip, Moroccan	Anthocharis belia	Marokkanischer Aurorafalter	Geel oranjetipje
Pasha, two-tailed	Charaxes jasius	Erdbeerbaumfalter	Aardbeiboomvlinder
Praying mantis, hooded	Empusa pennata	Kapuze-Gottesanbeterin*	Kapbidsprinkhaan*
Praying mantis	Mantis religiosa	Gottesanbeterin	Bidsprinkhaan
Ringlet, Piedmont	Erebia meolans	Gelbbindiger Mohrenfalter	Donkere erebia
Satyr, black	Satyrus actaea	Spanische Waldportier*	Kleine saterzandoog
Scarabs	Scarabaeidae	Blatthornkäfer	Mestkevers
Scolopendra	Scolopendra sp.	Riesenläufer/Gürtelskolopender	Scolopendra*
Scorpion, yellow	Buthus, occitanus	Gelbe Skorpion*	Gele schorpioen*
Scutigera	Scutigera sp.	Spinnenläufer	Scutigera*
Skipper, olive	Pyrgus serratulae	Schwarzbrauner Würfelfalter	Voorjaarsspikkeldikkopje
Skipper, silver-spotted	Hesperia comma	Komma-Dickkopffalter	Kommavlinder
Skipper, yellow-banded	Pyrgus sidae	Graubrauner Dickkopffalter	Geelbandspikkeldikkopje
Swallowtail	Papilio machaon	Schwalbenschwanz	Koninginnepage
Swallowtail, scarce	Iphiclides podalirius	Segelfalter	Koningspage
Tarantula	Lycosa narbonensis	Tarantula	Tarantula
Turtoiseshell, large	Nymphalis polychloros	Grosser Fuchs	Grote vos
White, Esper's marbeled	Melanargia russiae	Südliches Schachbrett	Zuidelijk dambordje
White, green-striped	Euchloe belemia	Grüngestreifter Weissling	Gestreept marmerwitje
White, Spanish marbled	Melanargia ines	Spanisches Schachbrett	Moors dambordje